IMAGES
of America

LOS ANGELES'S
KOREATOWN

Three flags—the California Bear Flag, the American flag, and the South Korean flag—fly in Koreatown in 1989. (Los Angeles Public Library.)

ON THE COVER: This is the Third Annual Young Korean Academy (*Hung Sa Dan*) in 1916 at 106 North Figueroa Street on Bunker Hill. The initials "Y.K.A." are painted on the porch beam above the spandrel. Chang Ho Ahn is the mustached figure in the front row, and his wife, Heyryon Ahn, is on the far right holding her daughter, Susan. Her son, Philson, is standing beside her. (Korean American Digital Archive.)

IMAGES
of America

LOS ANGELES'S
KOREATOWN

Katherine Yungmee Kim

ARCADIA
PUBLISHING

Published by Arcadia Publishing
Charleston, South Carolina

Library of Congress Control Number: 2011921613

For all general information, please contact Arcadia Publishing:
Telephone 843-853-2070
Fax 843-853-0044
E-mail sales@arcadiapublishing.com
For customer service and orders:
Toll-Free 1-888-313-2665

Visit us on the Internet at www.arcadiapublishing.com

*For my parents, Simyung Kim and Kija Sohn Kim, who emigrated
from Korea on September 3, 1955, and June 25, 1966, respectively.*

CONTENTS

FOREWORD

Koreatown is a great success story in the city of Los Angeles. Its legacy stands as not only a launching pad for the American Dreams of Korean immigrants in Los Angeles, but it has also set the mark for what an ethnic community can be in a large, metropolitan American city.

Following the Koreatown model, other immigrant communities have since carved out a piece of this great city from which to draw their American identity and build a distinct community. Just look at Thai Town, Little Armenia, Little Ethiopia, and Little Bangladesh—all have followed the lead of Koreatown. It is an economic force, an engine of commerce that has helped Los Angeles become the crossroads of the Pacific Rim.

Los Angeles's Koreatown is the largest in the United States, with more than 46,000 Korean Americans and Korean immigrants living here. That is more than four percent of all Koreans living in America. But Koreatown is also a melting pot. More than half of Koreatown residents are Hispanic. And whites, African Americans, Filipinos, and other Asian groups also call the area home.

Koreatown is a thriving, dynamic, and diverse community that looks a lot like Los Angeles itself. You could call Koreatown a microcosm of the city as a whole.

But what I like most about Koreatown is what it says about Los Angeles, how the city welcomes people from all over the world to come and make their dreams a reality. It shows Los Angeles at its finest, an outward-looking megalopolis, building on the varied strengths and creativity of all of its diverse populations, making it possible for immigrant groups to take pride in the neighborhoods they live in. In turn, those immigrants renovate, restore, and revitalize areas that may have been abandoned as others moved out to the suburbs.

Koreatown today is much more than an idea. It is a place fixed in the realities of city life and has become a potent symbol of what it means to be an immigrant in Los Angeles, and America. *Gamsahamnida!*

— Tom LaBonge
Councilmember, 4th District

ACKNOWLEDGMENTS

Los Angeles's Koreatown would never have come to fruition without the generous time, knowledge, and insight of many individuals and organizations. I am grateful to Joy Kim, curator of the Korean Heritage Library, USC; Dr. Ken Klein, head of the East Asian Library, USC; Sandy Close, executive director, Pacific News Service; and Johng Ho Song, executive director, Koreatown Youth and Community Center.

Tremendous gratitude goes to Susan Ahn Cuddy and Flip Cuddy, who provided photographs from the Helen Ahn Collection and inspired me to be exacting and honest.

My deepest appreciation goes to Dr. Eui-Young Yu, emeritus professor of sociology and founder and former director of the Center for Korean American and Korean Studies at UCLA, who was an inestimable friend, mentor, and beacon throughout my research and writing periods.

Thanks to Philip Levy, my uncle and owner of Bridge Street Books in Washington, DC, who sent me a copy of Ivan Light and Edna Bonacich's *Immigrant Entrepreneurs: Koreans in Los Angeles, 1965–1982*, which rekindled my passion for Korean American history.

My editors at Arcadia Publishing—Jerry Roberts, for seeing the value in this publication, and Debbie Seracini, for her patience, encouragements in Italian, and guidance—*grazie*.

Many people met and corresponded with me and offered their help, photographs, and time. I value everything I have learned from them: Lily Kim, the *Korea Times*; Dr. Sammy Lee; Todd Leitz; councilmember Tom LaBonge; Terri Garst, Los Angeles Public Library; Bill Yoon, Koreana Gifts and Art; Gloria Yoon; Carrie Yoon Kim Kwon; Carolyn Kim; Dr. Edward Yoon; Grace Yoon; Steve Yoon; Kelli Yoon; Dr. Edward Taehan Chang, Young Oak Kim Center for Korean American Studies, University of California, Riverside; Julie Ha, KoreAm; Jimmy Lee; K.W. Lee and Do Kim, K.W. Lee Center for Leadership; Ralph Ahn, Ann Ahn, Leslie Sang, Irvin Paik, Anne Kido, Alex Chang and the Korean American Pioneer Council; Grace Yoo, Korean American Coalition; Yonah Hong, the Community Redevelopment Agency of the City of Los Angeles; Paul Hyung Cho and Stuart Ahn, Los Angeles Korean United Methodist Church; Mary Connor, Korea Academy for Educators; Hi Duk Lee; Young Lee; Dr. David Yoo, Asian American Studies Center and Department, University of California, Los Angeles; Ann Watanabe-Rocco, Charles E. Young Research Library Department of Special Collections, UCLA; Carina Montoya Forsythe, Elizabeth Ruth-Abramian, Los Angeles Maritime Museum; Kathryn Shon; Herb Shon; Samuel Oh; Marsha Oh; Bethuel Chung; John Chung; Caroline Sung he Chung Takeda; and Grace Yi, Oriental Mission Church.

Special thanks go to my dear early readers: Kristy Kang, University of Southern California School of Cinematic Arts; Jim Aylward; Genie Chough and Kaitlin Solimine; and to Annie Sullivan, Seena Levy, Karena Levy, and Josh Parr.

I want to express my gratitude to my father for his kindness, my mother for her wisdom, and my brother for always understanding.

Above all, for Miles Akira, Dahlia Simone, Eitan Samuel, and Benjamin Paul—"more than tongue can tell."

All photographs from this collection are from the Korean American Digital Archive at USC's East Asian Library (KADA), the *Korea Times* photograph archives (KT), and the Helen Ahn Collection (HAC), unless otherwise noted.

INTRODUCTION

Los Angeles's Koreatown is the symbolic heart of Korean America. It is a spiritual and emotional center, a three-square-mile stretch of proliferating neon signs touting chicken barbecue and fishing supplies, 24-karat gold antiaging masks and Baptist churches, *soju* bars and tutoring centers. It is where Korean Angelenos conduct the quotidian—acupuncture appointments, business meetings, visa renewals, grocery shopping, banking. The mere expanse of Koreatown—it can seem just to go on and on for blocks—as it trickles toward Park La Brea, Crenshaw, and Silverlake, represents success in the "Beautiful Country," or *mi gook*, as America is called. Combined with the feeling of accomplishment that this city district represents are innate ethnic pride and an acknowledgement that assimilation "Ktown"-style means an appropriation of what it means to be an American.

Korean Americans in Koreatown have firmly established a very visible home base in the center of America's second-biggest metropolis. Los Angeles's Koreatown was the first of the world's Koreatowns—followed by sister districts in Flushing, Buenos Aires, Sydney, and Kazakhstan—beloved and built-up on such a grand scale for the overseas Korean diaspora. Koreatown heralded achievement for Koreans worldwide, as transplants, resilient, noble, and self-sufficient.

As Koreatown represents both a community and a geographic location, I wanted to honor the history of Koreans in Los Angeles, as well as the geographic location in the Mid-Wilshire District of Los Angeles and its storied past of Hollywood glamour and modernization.

The history of Koreans in Los Angeles has its beginnings on May 22, 1882, when the United States and Korea officially established diplomatic relations. Two years later, the first American missionaries—Presbyterian and Methodist—arrived, further sowing the seeds of Korean Christianity (Catholicism had been introduced in 1784). In 1885, a small, ostracized group of Korean political and social reformers arrived in San Francisco. Seo Jai-pil (also known as Philip Jaisohn) was among this group, arriving in 1888; he became the first Korean to obtain American citizenship.

Outside global powers and interests, Christianity and political activism would continue to be key characteristics of Korean American history.

In 1902, Chang Ho Ahn, a Korean philosopher and patriot, arrived in San Francisco with his wife, Heyryon Ahn. They were the first married Korean couple to arrive in the United States. At the time, there was a smattering of ginseng merchants and foreign students in the United States, but it wasn't until December of that year that 102 Korean laborers departed Korea for work on the Hawaiian sugarcane plantations. The shipload of immigrants—40 percent Christian—arrived in Hawaii on January 13, 1903, aboard the SS *Gaelic*. A climate of political instability, coupled with several poor harvests and famine in Korea, led to the exodus and mass immigration that (popularly) marks the arrival of Koreans in America.

The sugarcane workers, their picture brides, and a small community of students comprised the "First Wave" of Korean immigrants in America from 1885 to 1924, when the Asian Exclusion Act would prevent Asian immigration to the United States. During these four decades, only 7,000 Koreans lived in the United States.

From the 1900 to the 1920s, a small group of Koreans lived around Bunker Hill in Los Angeles, an area where nonwhites were allowed to reside, centering around a building that housed the Young Korean Academy, the Korean National Association Los Angeles branch headquarters and Chang Ho Ahn's family. The house—at 106 North Figueroa Street—was both a community center and stopping point for recent Korean immigrants, where they could receive lodging, guidance, and financial support in the new land. There was also a Methodist mission and rooming house in the neighborhood. A few small Korean-owned grocery stores sprouted in Bunker Hill, some of them short-lived.

The First Wave Korean Angelenos found employment as domestic help, grocery workers, waiters, or truck farmers. Many moved to the farming communities of Riverside, Reedley, Dinuba, Delano, and Stockton, harvesting fruit and produce.

The Wilshire District had its heyday in the 1920s and 1930s with the Brown Derby and Bullocks, the first neon sign in America, high-rises, and the Oscars at the Ambassador Hotel. It was the playground and residence of the stars from the Golden Age of Hollywood.

In the 1930s, the Korean community in Los Angeles eventually settled around the Jefferson Boulevard area, between Vermont and Normandie, near the University of Southern California campus. The "Old Koreatown" was where the Korean National Association headquarters was relocated from San Francisco in 1937, next to the Korean Presbyterian Church at 1374 Jefferson Boulevard.

Factionalism struck the Korean independence movement in the 1920s and 1930s, and abetted by the brutal Japanese colonial regime and its persecution of Korean independence fighters, its strength and abilities were hobbled. In the late 1930s, with Japanese expansion in Manchuria and China, the movement gained fresh momentum and the United Korean Committee organized Koreans in America during the Second World War. Ironically, it was the Japanese surrender that led to the end of Japanese rule in Korea. In 1945, two young American military officers arbitrarily set the 38th Parallel to divide Korea without Korean input or consultation, severing the Soviet-occupied North Korea from the US-occupied South Korea. In August 1948, Syngman Rhee was elected the first president of South Korea.

Meanwhile, the children of the First Wave were growing up American in Los Angeles. Many lived around Old Koreatown, where they attended schools such as the James A. Foshay Learning Center, Manual Arts High School, and Los Angeles High School. They graduated and matriculated into American universities and enlisted in the military. Many Korean Americans of this second generation joined the US Armed Forces. As children of the Korean independence movement, some felt compelled to "fight the Japs," but most of these veterans say they believed in the honor of serving their country as American citizens, despite the constant, egregious, and systemic discrimination they faced.

From 1950 to 1965, around 10,000 Koreans immigrated to America in the "Second Wave." The majority of these were Koreans orphaned during the Korean War (1950–1953), as well as the war brides of US soldiers who were stationed in South Korea. A small number were students and professional workers. During this time, many of the first Third Generation were born to Korean American baby boomers, and this community in Los Angeles painted a 1950s portrait of Korean American family life.

This era in Los Angeles saw the construction of the freeway system. The Wilshire area decentralized with the expansion of the freeways and the Watts Riots of 1965 further pummeled real estate and rents. The assassination of Robert F. Kennedy in the pantry of the Ambassador Hotel in 1968 was a tragic coda to the heralded Golden Era on Wilshire Boulevard.

The Hart-Cellar Act of 1965 brought upon the biggest change to the ethnic landscape of America, welcoming a preferential system based on family relationships and occupational skills, and Koreans began to arrive in droves, leaving behind a politically unstable country in the aftermath of the Korean War. Between 1965 and 1980, a total of 299,000 Koreans immigrated to the United States. Koreans in Los Angeles and Orange County accounted for 63 percent of Koreans in America in 1970. Lured by the incentive to pursue the American Dream, highly educated and with their families, the "Third Wave" of Korean Americans emigrated with the intention to stay—to build businesses and educate their children in their new homeland.

The confluence of the Watts Riots and the freeway decentralization triggered many who lived in the Wilshire Center area to move to the suburbs. Meanwhile, the number of Korean immigrants—in search of affordable housing and business opportunities—began to establish a community in the economically depressed area. Soon, the Old Koreatown on Jefferson Boulevard began to migrate towards Olympic Boulevard.

During the 1970s and 1980s, Korean real estate developers and highly educated immigrants—who faced discrimination and language barriers in the mainstream job market—opened hundreds of small businesses in the area. Koreatown's framework was established during this time, and civic organizations began to flourish, addressing and advocating for social service improvements in the community. Immigration peaked in 1987 with nearly 36,000 Koreans arriving in America that year alone.

Christian churches played an essential role throughout Korean American history, providing community services, social interaction, and financial aid. It is impossible to overlook their significance. There are more than 4,000 Korean churches in the United States—700 of them are located in Los Angeles. More than 70 percent of Korean immigrant families claim to be members of a congregation.

On April 29, 1992, the Korean American community suffered its "baptism of fire" during the Los Angeles riots. Six days of rioting and looting, centralized in Koreatown and exacerbated by the absence of police protection, led to the destruction of more than 2,000 Korean-owned businesses, amounting to over $400 million in damages.

The riots marked a turning point in the Korean American community—a sad, scarred, and pivotal moment when Korean Americans entered into the mainstream consciousness. While the community emerged with a determination to become more politically astute, many shop owners—already jaded from 14-hour workdays, threats to their safety, and racial animosity—retreated for the suburbs in San Fernando, Riverside, and Orange Counties.

The fear and loss of infrastructure left parts of the Koreatown area a veritable ghost town. But Korean American, South Korean, and other Asian investors instead saw an opportunity to expand development in North America. Multileveled condo-plexes, banks, shopping centers, and nightclubs emerged in the 1990s and 2000s. Changes to immigration laws in 1990 and 1996 favored wealthy Korean immigrants, who have migrated back and forth. Koreatown became popular for its after-hours bars, restaurants, and nightlife, but with the residue of the riots and one of the poorest communities in Los Angeles, the area suffered from the reputation—deserved or not—of being a high-crime area.

Demographically, the largest concentration—25 percent or 257,975—of Korean Americans live in the five-county (Los Angeles, Ventura, Orange, San Bernardino, and Riverside) area. Koreatown itself is home to more than 46,000 of these immigrants, but it boasts an incredibly diverse community. Around 52 percent are from Mexico and Central and Latin America, 20.1 percent are from Korea, 30 percent are white, and around five percent are African American and Filipino, respectively. But the area remains a paradox; while its exterior beholds ostentation and affluence, its reality is that 70 percent of its residents are part of the working-poor, and more than 70 percent are immigrants. More than 150,000 low-income people live and work in the neighborhood—one of the densest—and unfortunately, one of the least green—areas in the United States.

Koreatown received its belated official designation from the Los Angeles City Council on August 20, 2010. Two traditional Korean gates are being built on Olympic Boulevard—at Vermont and Western Avenues—to stand as welcoming sentries to the neighborhood. One of the biggest pushes is for redistricting, so that Koreatown will hopefully fall under two city councils as opposed to four (and one day, ideally under one) to consolidate and augment the community's strength, financial opportunities, and political power.

With its newly declared formal identity, Koreatown is reestablishing itself as a multicultural, socioeconomically diverse, and intergenerational community, uniting in its efforts to keep government funds locally distributed, to create more affordable housing, job growth, and career training, and to build bigger, safer, and better parks, community centers, and schools for its citizens.

One

THE FIRST WAVE

The *Los Angeles Times* Bicycle Club is pictured walking and riding bicycles north on Western Avenue from Pico Boulevard in 1895. Around 100,000 people lived in Los Angeles, though much of the land was still dirt roads and fields. That year, Henry Gaylord Wilshire announced his plan to create a 120-foot-wide gravel road through his 35-acre barley field. The four-block-long path was named Wilshire Boulevard. (KADA.)

This is an image of the famous SS *Gaelic* that carried the first boatload of 102 Korean immigrants from Nagasaki, Japan, to Honolulu, Hawaii. The boat arrived in Hawaii on January 13, 1903. There were 56 men (mostly bachelors), 21 women, and 25 children on board. Forty percent of the contract laborers were Christian, recruited by missionaries to work on the plantations. (KT.)

The passport of Korean patriots Chang Ho Ahn and his wife, Heyryon Lee (also known as Helen Lee Ahn), documents their entry into San Francisco—via Vancouver, Seattle, Hawaii, and Japan—on October 14, 1902. Ahn and Lee were the first married Korean couple to immigrate to the United States. During their journey across the Pacific, Ahn chose the pen name *Dosan*, meaning, "island mountain." (HAC.)

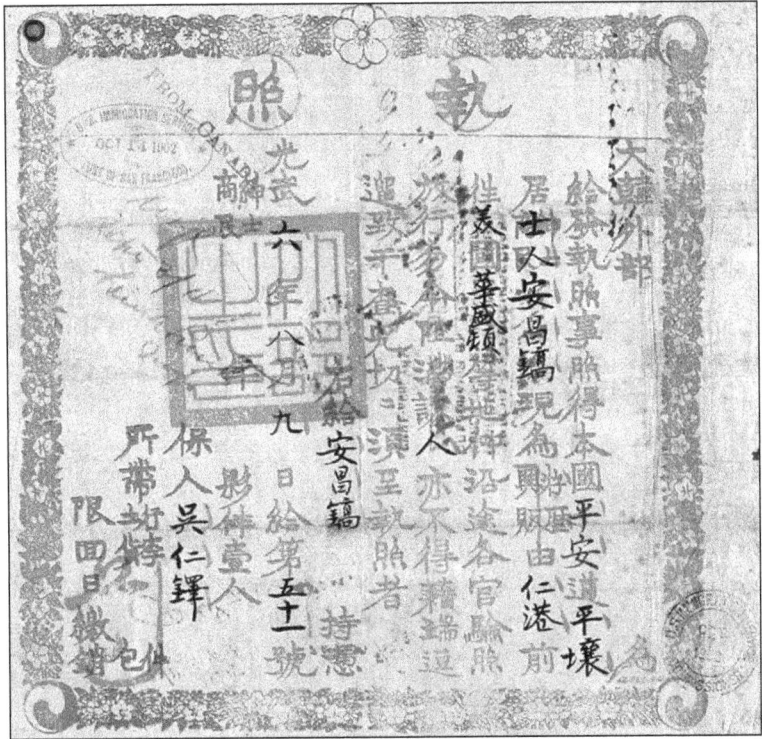

Eui Suk Char's (also known as Emsen Charr) Korean passport, issued in 1904, documents his solo journey to America at the age of 10. Char arrived in San Francisco, via Hawaii, in 1905. His 1996 autobiography, *The Golden Mountain*, details his life from 1895 to 1960 as a Korean American First Wave immigrant. (KADA.)

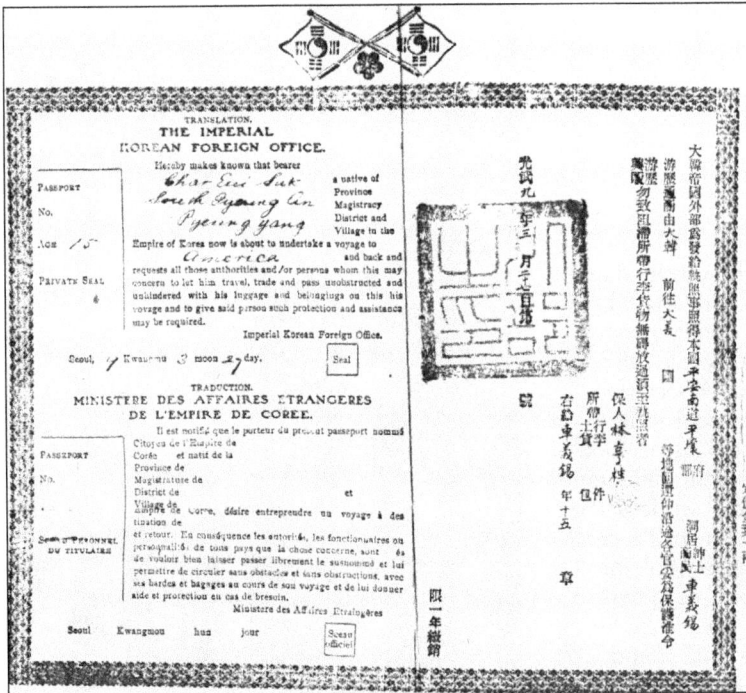

Choong Sup Park left Korea in 1902 for work in Hawaii on the sugarcane and pineapple plantations. His wife—and childhood sweetheart—Chung Kyung Lee, joined him in 1915; that year, they wed in San Francisco. Between 1903 and 1905, 7,226 immigrants from Korea arrived in Hawaii; more than 6,000 were male adults. By 1910, the Korean population in Hawaii decreased, as 2,000 had journeyed to the mainland and another 1,000 returned to Korea. (KADA.)

Like the few thousand who ventured from Hawaii to the mainland, Park arrived in 1905 via steamship in San Francisco, where Korean organizations such as the Korean Mutual Assistance Association (*Kongnip hyophoe*), a precursor to the influential Korean National Association (*Kung Min Hoe*), helped recent immigrants with employment and social services. Park moved to Riverside, where he had a small ranch, a produce store, and a wholesale produce business. Park and Lee moved to Los Angeles in 1932 and lived there for six years before moving to McFarland, where they had a small farm. (KADA.)

Above is the Korean Methodist Episcopal Mission located at 1519 Hill Street on Bunker Hill in Los Angeles. The mission—founded in 1904 with a congregation of 25 men, mostly students and laborers—provided housing, employment advice, a Korean-language church service, Bible classes, Sunday school, and English-language lessons. Protestant Christians were heavily involved in the movement for Korean Independence. (Los Angeles Unified Korean Methodist Church.)

Florence Sherman was the founder and superintendent of the Korean Methodist Episcopal Mission. She and her husband, the medical missionary Dr. Harry Sherman, lived in Korea from 1898 to 1900 and befriended influential Korean independence movement activists, such as Hugh Cynn and Syngman Rhee. After Harry's death, Cynn lived with Florence while he attended the University of Southern California. (LAUKMC.)

Hugh Heung-Wo Cynn was a graduate of Pai Chai Academy, one of the oldest modern universities in Korea. Pai Chai was founded by Henry Appenzeller, a Methodist missionary who helped introduce Protestant Christianity to Korea in 1885. Cynn, a Christian nationalist, was the first pastor at the Korean Methodist Episcopal Mission from 1904 to 1911. He returned to Korea and became principal of Pai Chai and general-secretary of the YMCA in Korea. (KADA.)

Soonkey Rhee arrived in Hawaii in 1905, made his way to Los Angeles in 1907, and graduated from Occidental Academy, a preparatory school at Occidental College, in 1910. His wife, Eunkee Chun, arrived on Angel Island in 1912. His first son, Sammy Lee, was born in 1920 in Fresno, where the family had a truck farming business. They moved to Bunker Hill, where Rhee opened a small grocery, and eventually settled in Highland Park. (LAPL.)

This photograph, taken between 1910 and 1925, is of South Vermont Avenue in the Wilshire Center district. From the turn of the century to 1915, the four-block Wilshire Boulevard was expanded and paved from Westlake Park to the ocean. The entire city, boosted by the railroad and railway systems, was rapidly industrializing and growing. The 1910 census counted 319,200 residents; in 1920, the number jumped to 576,700. (USC Special Collections.)

Chang Ho Ahn moved from San Francisco to Riverside in the fall of 1903. He had just established the first Korean social organization—the Friendship Society (*Chinmokhoe*)—in San Francisco to establish Korean rights. He also systematized the ginseng merchants' territories there after witnessing a dispute between two sellers. In Riverside, he organized the citrus grove workers, building community and morale, and he founded the Korean Mutual Assistance Association (*Kongnip hyophoe*) in 1905. Ahn returned to San Francisco over the next few years, building the Mutual Assistance Association. He would also journey to Korea in 1907 and traveled through Manchuria, China, and Russia, before returning to Los Angeles via London and New York in 1911. It was during his trip abroad that Korea was annexed by Japan on August 22, 1910. Ahn was the first leader of all of the international branches of the Korean National Association, which had been formed in 1909. It would be the leading governing body for Koreans in America and for Korean independence. This photograph of Ahn in the Alta Cuesta orange groves of Riverside was taken in 1912. (HAC.)

Pachappa Lane in Riverside in 1911 housed Korean citrus grove workers in several dormitories. After Koreans moved to the mainland from Hawaii, many of them landed in San Francisco, Los Angeles, or in one of the Korean farming communities in Riverside, Dinuba, Reedley, Delano, Willows, Stockton, and Fresno, among others. Hundreds of Korean workers would arrive for the summer harvest season to work on the farms. Churches and organizations were established in these towns. (HAC.)

The Korean Band in Claremont in 1916 was the first Korean band in the United States. After 1910, about 540 "refugee students" left Korea via China. They were granted asylum by the United States. A "Student Clubhouse" was built in Claremont, where Koreans attended elementary, junior high, and high school, regardless of age. The clubhouse provided room and board and was close to farming communities. It closed in 1917. (HAC.)

This photograph shows automobile traffic at the intersection of First Street and Figueroa Street on Bunker Hill around 1915. The Young Korean Academy (*Hung Sa Dan*) building and Ahn family house is the peaked Victorian on the top right of the image. "Korean Society Site—Chang Ho House" is written on the image. A small grocery is on the right, advertising "Beers and Wines." (KADA.)

Three out of four of the Ahn children are pictured on the porch of the 106 North Figueroa Street house. Philson (right, b. 1912), Susan (left, b. 1915), and Soorah (in the high chair, b. 1917) were among the first of the second-generation Korean Americans. Their older brother, Philip (b. 1905), was believed to be the first child of Korean descent born in the United States. (HAC.)

A group of men are sitting informally on the flatbed of a pickup truck at 106 North Figueroa Street in 1919. As there was no Korean consulate at the time, the Ahn family house served as a community center—a rooming house, dining hall, and gathering place for the Koreans who lived in and visited Southern California. The house was also the headquarters of the Young Korean Academy (*Hung Sa Dan*), which was founded by Chang Ho Ahn on May 13, 1913, in San Francisco. The YKA was a moral and character-building organization established to create virtuous, socially conscious, and healthy citizens. The *Hung Sa Dan* constitution sought to uphold "the highest human ideals" and to "dedicate ourselves to our country and people." (LAPL.)

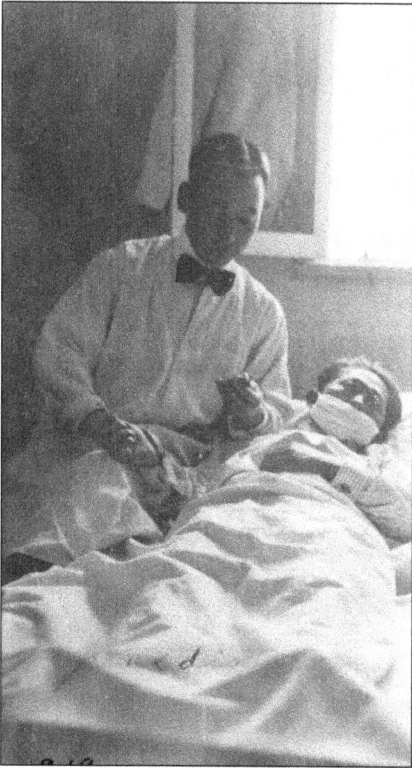

Jang Ho Hahn tends to a sick friend in 1919, possibly in Dinuba or Reedley, two farming towns with Korean American communities. Hahn was an instructor of Chong Lim Kim's Korean Aviation School in Willows, California, and Yongman Park's Military Institute in Hastings, Nebraska. (KADA.)

There was a slow but steady trickling of student immigrants from Korea in the 1920s and 1930s. Students started arriving in the late 1800s, and many of those who signed up to work on the Hawaiian plantations were students. Seventy-five percent of the students who arrived between 1899 and 1909 graduated from college, and more than half stayed in the United States. This portrait was taken on July 2, 1921. (KADA.)

The character of Clara from Gloria Hahn's (also known as Kim Ronyoung) fictional account of the Korean American First Wave generation, *Clay Walls*, was based on Po Eun Lee. She was also the mother of Lucille Lee Ahn, who married Philson Ahn. This photograph is from the early 1920s. Clara was a first-generation picture bride, married to a member of the Korean National Association, and dressed in Western fashions. From 1910 to 1924, 1,066 Korean picture brides arrived in Hawaii; around 100 entered the continental United States during the same time period. Many of them were quite young (some were 17), but many of them were educated. From 1901 to 1903, only three Korean women entered the United States. From 1903 to 1910, only 677 women entered, leaving the ratio of men to women 10:1. After the picture brides' arrival, and the coming-of-age of the 250 or so girls who had immigrated as children, the ratio was reduced to 3:1.5 after World War II. (KADA.)

Pictured is Do Yen Kim (left) and Yong Ho Yoon's wedding in 1915 in San Francisco. Kim was a picture bride. The Yoons moved to Los Angeles in 1938. The wedding photograph below of an unidentified Korean immigrant couple in the 1920s shows the bride in a flapper-style headdress. Whether or not she is a picture bride is unknown. Because of the disproportionate number of men to women, many women—married or not—were pursued as partners. Most of the 2,000 women who had arrived in the United States before the 1924 Asian Exclusion Act married and had children. However, at this time, there were still 3,000 bachelors. The Asian Exclusion Act set a quota for immigrants to be limited to two percent of the country's population in the United States in 1890. This act all but prohibited Korean entry into the United States; its goal was to "maintain the racial preponderance of the basic strain on our people and thereby to stabilize the ethnic composition of the population." (Both, KADA.)

The International Institute in Los Angeles was founded in 1914 as a branch of the Young Women's Christian Association. The institute's mission was to "serve women and girls coming from Europe and the Orient and to assist the foreign communities in their adjustment to life in this country." Korean women immigrants are pictured in 1922 attending an English-language class that the institute provided. (LAPL.)

This is a portrait of the 11th Assembly of the Young Korean Academy in front of Robinson's department store on Seventh Street in downtown Los Angeles in 1924. Chang Ho Ahn is in the front row, in the middle of the three men in sashes. (HAC.)

From 1913 to 1919, Chang Ho Ahn traveled to Hawaii, Mexico, San Francisco, and Shanghai as a leader in the Korean independence movement. After the March 1, 1919, uprising in Korea against Japanese rule, Ahn—described as "the most skilled conciliator and gifted institution-builder"—left for Shanghai where he helped establish the Korean Provisional Government of the Republic of Korea (KPG), a central organization that joined with the Provisional Governments from Vladivostok and Seoul. The Provisional Government proclaimed Korean independence from Japan and coordinated armed movements against the Japanese. Many of the Korean organizations in the United States fighting for Korean independence provided the funding for the Provisional Government. It was estimated that more than $200,000 or $30 per person—one month's salary—was sent to China. This photograph was taken in Los Angeles in 1919. (HAC.)

A pensive shot of Chang Ho Ahn in 1925 was taken on the porch of 106 North Figueroa Street. At the time, the Provisional Government-in-exile was beset by internal rifts and factionalism. Ahn resigned in 1921; Yongman Park, another key leader, who had formed a military school in Nebraska, opposed the KPG; and Syngman Rhee, the first KPG president, was impeached for misuse of authority. Rhee created a separate organization, the Comrade Society (*Tongjihoe*), in Hawaii in 1921. There were disputes that divided the independence movement as to whether to align with the United States or the Soviet Union, as well as conflicting ideologies of militarism versus diplomacy. (HAC.)

Philip Jaisohn (left) and Chang Ho Ahn met in Los Angeles on July 27, 1925, to discuss Korean independence. Jaisohn arrived in the United States in 1885 as a political exile. In 1888, he became the first Korean to be naturalized as an American citizen and, in 1892, the first Korean to obtain a medical degree (Johns Hopkins University). It is unclear as to how he obtained the citizenship benefit, as it was given only to "free white persons," but he was married to an American woman, Muriel Armstrong, who was the niece of Pres. James Buchanan. He returned to Korea and established the first newspaper printed in Korean, the *Independent*, and remained a leader and educator in the Korean independence movement, largely from his home base in Philadelphia where he was also a medical researcher. (HAC.)

Chang Ho Ahn departed San Pedro on the SS *Sonoma* (pictured). The boat broke down, and he was waylaid in San Francisco before arriving in Shanghai—via Hawaii, Fiji, Samoa, Australia, and Hong Kong—on May 16, 1926. In Shanghai, Ahn was arrested by the Japanese in 1932 and was imprisoned in Korea. After being released, he was again arrested and put in prison in 1937 and died in Seoul in 1938. After this departure, he never returned to Los Angeles, nor did he see his family again. (HAC.)

Children are assembled for a photograph in front of their Korean-language schools in Los Angeles in 1926. The school pictured above was located at a residence on Thirty-seventh Street. (KADA.)

A family portrait of Syung Min Lee, his wife, Esther, and their adopted daughter, Helen Hong, was taken in a studio in Los Angeles in 1920. At the time, Helen was around eight years old. The 1920 census counted 89 Koreans living in Los Angeles; 18 of them were children. (LAPL.)

Esther Kim and her children, Bill and Linda Herr, were photographed on the front lawn of their Los Angeles home on Thirty-seventh Street in the West Adams district in 1929. Esther Kim's husband, Raymond Herr, was one of the most active supporters of Syngman Rhee. By this time, the numbers of Korean women in the community had risen, and as of 1924, there were approximately 1,900 Korean families in the United States. (LAPL.)

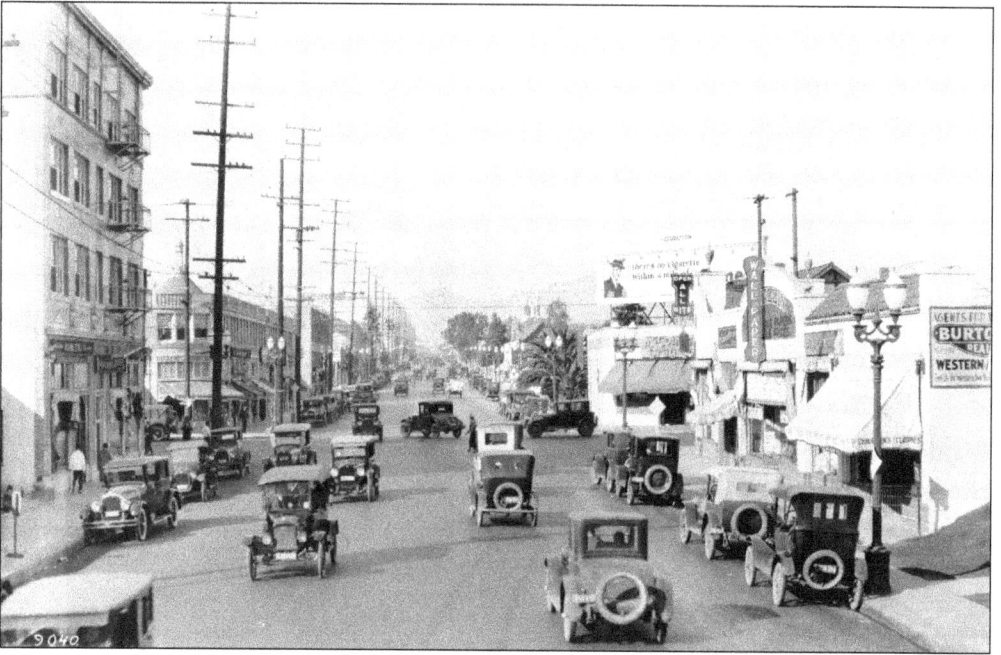

The Automobile Age arrived in Wilshire Center. In 1920, about 67,000 pleasure cars were recorded in Los Angeles. This photograph of Western Avenue looking north from Sixth Street in 1924 shows the area as a bustling commercial district, with advertisements for Camel cigarettes and a sign for the Owl Drug Store. (USC.)

This is the intersection of Washington Boulevard and Vermont Avenue around 1925–1930. Streetcars, automobiles, and pedestrians travel the street and signs hail California Bank and Bennett Drugs. The West Coast Theatre (right) was a Spanish Colonial film palace that opened in 1925 with 2,300 seats, a stage, and an organ. (USC.)

Opened on New Year's Day in 1921, the Ambassador Hotel cemented Wilshire Boulevard's grand reputation during its golden age. Built on 23 acres of a former dairy farm, the hotel was a playground for socialites with its golf course, bowling alley, horse stables, and shops. The Academy Awards were held at its Fiesta Room and famed Cocoanut Grove six times from 1930 to 1943. (USC.)

The original Brown Derby restaurant, with its hat-shaped roof and lore of the original Cobb salad, was opened in 1926 across the street from the Ambassador Hotel. Located at 3427 Wilshire Boulevard, it was a popular casual dining spot with such menu items as corned beef hash for 30¢ and a bottle of Coca-Cola for 10¢. (USC.)

This is a photograph of the northwest corner of Wilshire Boulevard and Vermont Avenue c. 1930. There is a flower stand in front of the brick church, and automobiles travel in every direction. The site is now the Wilshire/Vermont Station for the Los Angeles County Metro Rail System. It services the red and purple lines and houses the two longest escalators in California. (USC.)

The Wilshire Boulevard Temple—with its Byzantine dome, black marble, and gold inlay interior—was dedicated in 1929 on the corner of Wilshire Boulevard and Normandie Avenue. It was originally located at the intersection of Temple Street and Broadway and at a second location at Hope Street and Ninth Street downtown. It is the oldest temple in Los Angeles. (USC.)

Two

OLD KOREATOWN

In the 1930s, the Korean community in Los Angeles migrated from Bunker Hill towards the West Adams district near the University of Southern California. Los Angeles was the first city to apply racially restrictive covenants in real estate in the 1920s, which segregated white neighborhoods from people of color. Yin Kim is photographed in his sweater from Foshay Junior High School, where many of the second generation Korean Americans attended, in 1930. (LAPL.)

Susan Ahn Cuddy (second row, fourth from left) is pictured with her homeroom class at Central Junior High School, located where Los Angeles City College currently exists on Vermont Avenue. In this April 1930 photograph, Cuddy is the homeroom class president. (HAC.)

Three sisters pose for the camera on the beach in Los Angeles on July 4, 1931. From left to right are Helen Hong, Sunda (Hur) Hahn, and Frances (Hur) Hahn. Frances was married to Jang Ho Hahn. (KADA.)

Soonkey Rhee, photographed at his house at 5711 York Boulevard in Highland Park, was a childhood friend and supporter of Syngman Rhee. Neighbors said they did not want "Chinks" or "Japs" in the neighborhood, but the German immigrant who owned a grocery store connected to their house defended the Rhees and rented to them. Due to the Great Depression and the opening of an A&P grocery store across the street, Rhee's wife, Eunkee, opened a chop suey restaurant within the grocery store to make a living. (LAPL.)

Mary Lee Shon was the daughter of Soonkey Rhee and sister of Olympic diver Sammy Lee. She was a triple major at the University of Southern California, with degrees in sociology, religious education, and social work. She was one of the first Korean Americans to graduate from USC. Shon was a lifelong educator in Southern California and founder of the Korean American Educators Association. The eponymous Mary Lee Shon Education Center opened at the Wilton Place Elementary School in Los Angeles in 2001. (KADA.)

BANQUET
TO
KOREAN OLYMPIC PLAYERS
GIVEN BY
THE TWO-EIGHT CLUB AND THE YOUNG KOREAN NATION
THE ELITE LOS ANGELES, CALIFORNIA. JU.

A banquet was given in the honor of the Korean Olympians in the 1932 Games of the X Olympiad held in Los Angeles. The Two-Eight Club was one of the first Korean American clubs organized in the United States. It was created by some of the older members of the second generation when

they were teenagers. The social club was launched in 1928 with 28 members—thus the name. The Two-Eight Club and the Young Korean National Association sponsored this dinner at the Elite on July 31, 1932. (KADA.)

The Young Korean National Association was a subsidiary organization of the Korean National Association, with a membership of approximately 50 second-generation Korean Americans. This photograph is of a dinner dance in Los Angeles in 1936, where members across California convened to give speeches and socialize. The purpose of the organization was to build community and encourage patriotism to the Provisional Government. (KADA.)

Four Korean men work in the hotel industry in 1935. Many of the Koreans in Los Angeles worked in the fruit and produce industries, in laundries and restaurants, and as domestic help. At this time, not a single Korean in Los Angeles County was in the professions of law, engineering, dentistry, education, or social work. (LAPL.)

The 18th Assembly of the Young Korean Academy was held at the University of Southern California in 1931. This photograph was taken in front of the arches at the Seeley Wintersmith Mudd Memorial Hall of Philosophy. (HAC.)

The Korean National Association (KNA) kept information on the Korean American community in a journal titled the *National Diary*. These documents from 1931 show a page recording births, deaths, and marriages. The notebook also contained meeting information, accounting figures, steamship and passenger names, dates of journey, and other KNA-related memoranda. (KADA.)

In 1936, the Los Angeles Korean Methodist Church, South was located at 1416 Thirty-seventh Drive near Normandie Avenue in Old Koreatown. After the Hill Street mission closed in 1912, the church entered what it described as a "period of wandering in the wilderness," marked by interdenominational conflicts that were exacerbated by Korean nationalist politics. Eventually

in 1930, the church was renamed and reorganized as an entity of the Methodist Episcopal Church, South. Within a year, the church would move again to a nearby African American Seventh-Day Adventist Church—one of many moves that came before and after, as the church searched for a permanent home. (KADA.)

Above is Shungnak "Sung Nak" Luke Kim's 1937 immigrant identification card issued by the US Department of Labor. It states his country of birth as "Chosen" and his nationality as "Japanese." It lists his arrival at the port in San Pedro on February 15, 1937, on the SS *Taiyo Maru*. (KADA.)

The immigration visa for Shungnak Kim, his wife, Chong Ok Yun, and his four children—George (b. 1933), Grace (b. 1936), Paul (b. 1926), and Samuel (b. 1935)—was issued on January 8, 1937, in "Seoul, Chosen" by the American vice consul. The Japanese passport is stamped with the words "Imperial Japanese Government." (KADA.)

大日本帝國外務大臣 從三位勲一等有田八郎

第３２０６７６號

昭和十二年一月六日

右ハ布教ノ為北米合衆國ヘ（以下余白）

赴ク二付通路故障ナク旅行セシメ且必要ナル保護扶助ヲ與ヘラレムヿヲ其ノ筋ノ諸官ニ希望ス

金聖樂 明治三十六年四月二十六日生
同伴者
妻 尹宗王 明治三十六年四月五日生
長男 利國 大正十五年九月一日生
二男 亨國 昭和八年九月十二日生
三男 元國 昭和十年一月二十三日生
長女 貞淑 昭和十二年十二月四日生

The passport issued by the Imperial Japanese Government for Shungnak Kim states that he would be entering the United States "for missionary work accompanying his family." The family is recorded as a "Japanese subject" and Shungnak Kim lists his occupation as "pastor." It also notes the family's height and "physical peculiarities." Shungnak Luke Kim arrived in Los Angeles when he was 34 years old and served the Los Angeles Korean community as the pastor for the Korean Presbyterian Church on Jefferson Boulevard from 1938 to 1959. He returned to Korea in 1959 and served as president of Soong Sil University in Seoul. (KADA.)

ORIGINAL ORIGINAL
DEPARTMENT OF STATE
OF
THE UNITED STATES OF AMERICA

AMERICAN CONSULATE AT Seoul, Chosen

January 8, 1937.

THIS CARD IS ISSUED FOR THE IDENTIFICATION OF THE PERSON WHOSE NAME APPEARS ON THE REVERSE SIDE AS THE BEARER OF NON QUOTA-QUOTA IMMIGRATION VISA No. - 15 -
Section 4 (d) ISSUED BY THIS CONSULATE.
THIS CARD IS NOT TRANSFERABLE AND WILL NOT BE VALID FOR PURPOSES OF IDENTIFICATION IN THE UNITED STATES UNTIL DULY SIGNED BY AN IMMIGRANT INSPECTOR AT A PORT OF ENTRY TO THE UNITED STATES.

849644 Vice CONSUL OF THE U. S. A.

The Korean Presbyterian Church located at 1374 Jefferson Boulevard in Old Koreatown was built and open for services on May 1, 1938, under the leadership of Rev. Sung Nak Kim. The church still stands in its original location. The much larger Korean United Presbyterian Church was built in 1983, adjoining the smaller brick building. (KADA.)

The Korean National Association (KNA) relocated its headquarters in 1937 from San Francisco to Los Angeles. The new KNA building was completed in 1938 at 1386 Jefferson Boulevard, next to the Korean Presbyterian Church, where it still remains. The presence of both buildings solidified the area's Korean presence and Los Angeles as a center for Korean independence activity in the United States. (KADA.)

46

Chang Ho Ahn died at the age of 60 on March 10, 1938, at the Kyungsung Hospital in Seoul after being tortured and imprisoned by the Japanese at the Sodaemun Prison. He had contracted tuberculosis, pleurisy, and peritonitis. It was reported that the Japanese guards put crushed glass in his meals in the prison. The Korean National Association held a memorial at the United Methodist Church (now the United University Church on the USC campus) to honor the Korean patriot, social reformer, independence activist, and leader of the Korean American community in Los Angeles on March 20, 1938. (KADA.)

Sung Taik Lim stands in his grocery market in Whittier, possibly Dinuba. Many Korean Californians were fruit sellers and grocery owners. Other occupations included domestic help, farm laborers, grape pickers, truck farmers, railroad and mine workers, and hotel employees. (KADA.)

The Gaylord Apartments, a 14-story structure built by Gaylord Wilshire in 1921 on Wilshire Boulevard and Kenmore Avenue, is pictured in 1938. Sally's Home Made Cuisine and the Wilshire Boulevard Temple are in the distance. (USC.)

The Wiltern, built by Henri de Roulet in 1931, is a beautiful Art Deco building with verdigris terra-cotta tiles. The Zigzag Moderne building was originally called the Warner Bros. Western Theater, and it closed one year after it opened due to the Great Depression. When it reopened in the mid-1930s, it was renamed the Wiltern. (USC.)

This aerial view of Wilshire Boulevard looks west from Commonwealth Avenue in the 1930s. Bullocks Wilshire, built in 1929, is seen on the left with its 241-foot tower. On the north side of the street is a sign for the Gaylord Apartments. Film stars, such as Norma Talmadge with her namesake apartments on Wilshire and Normandie, and leading families, such as the Van Nuys, moved into the high-rises and affluent residential neighborhoods (Windsor Square, Fremont Place, Hancock Park) near the boulevard. I. Magnin opened in 1939 at Wilshire Boulevard and New Hampshire Avenue as the first fully electric building in the United States. (USC.)

This photograph is a window into the social climate at the time; Pauline Cho is being deported with her son on December 2, 1938, for breaking anti-miscegenation laws. It was not until 1948 that the California State Supreme Court ruled the California anti-miscegenation statute was a violation of the 14th Amendment to the US Constitution. California was the first state since 1887 to repeal this law. (KADA.)

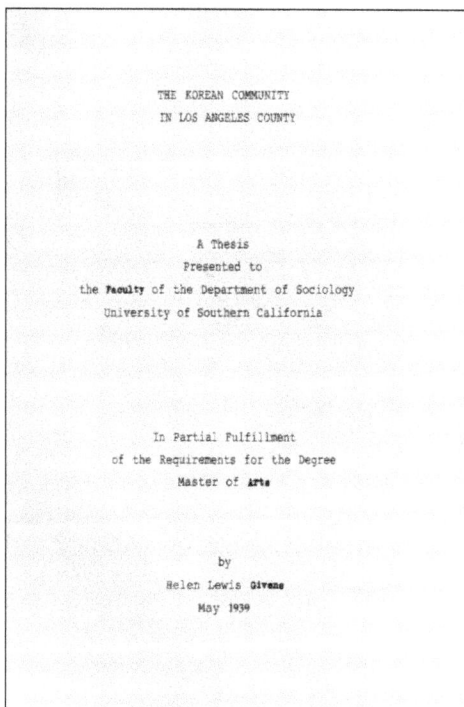

THE KOREAN COMMUNITY
IN LOS ANGELES COUNTY

A Thesis
Presented to
the Faculty of the Department of Sociology
University of Southern California

In Partial Fulfillment
of the Requirements for the Degree
Master of Arts

by
Helen Lewis Givens
May 1939

In May 1939, Helen Lewis Givens presented the "Korean Community in Los Angeles County" to partially fulfill her requirements for her master of arts degree in sociology from the University of Southern California. This seminal paper documented the organizations, family life, customs, and politics of the Korean community in Los Angeles at the time. (KADA.)

Three

WORLD WAR II, THE KOREAN WAR, AND THE SECOND WAVE

Anne Kido, a member of the Korean American Pioneer Council, recalls this protest in Los Angeles in the late 1930s. She was the little girl in braids holding the sign that reads "Korea Fights for Independence." The Korean American independence movement was revitalized in the face of Japanese imperialism at the advent of World War II. (KADA.)

United Korean Committee in America

1868 WEST JEFFERSON BOULEVARD
LOS ANGELES, CALIFORNIA

REGISTRATION OF RESIDENT KOREANS

I. Name: M _Mr._ _Kook_ _Oh_
     (Mr., Mrs., Miss) (first name) (middle name) (last name)

II. Address:
    A. _1287 W. 36th St. Los Angeles, Cal._
       (St. address or R.R.)   (city)   (county)   (state)

    P. O. Box Address _____

III. I was born on _7 - 17 - 1876_. Birthplace _Choong Chung, Korea_
     (month) (day) (year)

IV. Dependents:

    A. (Wife ~~or husband~~) _Kyungsim Oh_ Age _69_ _Pyado, Korea_
                                   (name)   Birthplace

    B. Names of children:
       _____ Age_____ Sex_____ _____
       _____ Age_____ Sex_____ _____
       _____ Age_____ Sex_____ _____
       _____ Age_____ Sex_____ _____

V. Occupation: _____

    A. Business address: _Same_

    Date of registration _4-27_ , 19_42_

    Signature of registrant: _Kook Oh_

The Alien Registration Act—also known as the Smith Act—was passed on June 29, 1940, and required all alien residents over 14 years of age to document their address, profession, and political beliefs. It was enacted to undermine Communism in America. The United Korean Committee and the Korean Commission in Washington, DC, oversaw the registration for the Korean American community. (Both, KADA.)

United Korean Committee in America

1868 WEST JEFFERSON BOULEVARD
LOS ANGELES, CALIFORNIA

REGISTRATION OF RESIDENT KOREANS

I. Name: MR _Chi_ _Duk_ _Pai_
     (Mr., Mrs., Miss) (first name) (middle name) (last name)

II. Address: _225 N. Oline St. Los Angeles, California_
    A.
       (St. address or R.R.)   (city)   (county)   (state)

    P. O. Box Address _____

III. I was born on _Aug. 17 1870_. Birthplace _Kyung Sang, Korea_
     (month) (day) (year)

IV. Dependents: _None_

    A. (Wife or husband) _____ Age_____   Birthplace

    B. Names of children:
       _____ Age_____ Sex_____ _____
       _____ Age_____ Sex_____ _____
       _____ Age_____ Sex_____ _____
       _____ Age_____ Sex_____ _____

V. Occupation: _Laborer_

    A. Business address: _____

    Date of registration _April 27_ , 19_42_

    Signature of registrant: _Chi Duk Pai_

The Young Korean Convention was held in Los Angeles during Easter break in 1940. Young Korean Americans from San Francisco, Oakland, Dinuba, Reedley, and Los Angeles sponsored this gathering, and many of them stayed in the USC dormitories, which were vacant due to the holidays. It was the first time that the second-generation Korean Americans in California came together. English- and Korean-speaking contests, debates, and basketball tournaments were held, along with a banquet and dance at the Wilshire Ebell Theatre. The older Korean women in the community served meals at the Korean Presbyterian Church. (KADA.)

Samples of a bumper sticker, lapel button, and pocket identification card are displayed on a paper with the United Korean Committee for America letterhead. The United Korean Committee was the umbrella organization for all Korean independence groups. It sent money to the Korean Provisional Government and the Korean Commission. It also raised more than $25,000 for President Roosevelt and another several hundred dollars for the Red Cross. Koreans in America—often mistaken for the Japanese Americans who were being sent to "War Relocation" or internment camps at the time—wore these pins and carried the ID cards to differentiate themselves as Korean, to advocate for Korean independence, and to ally with the United States. (KADA.)

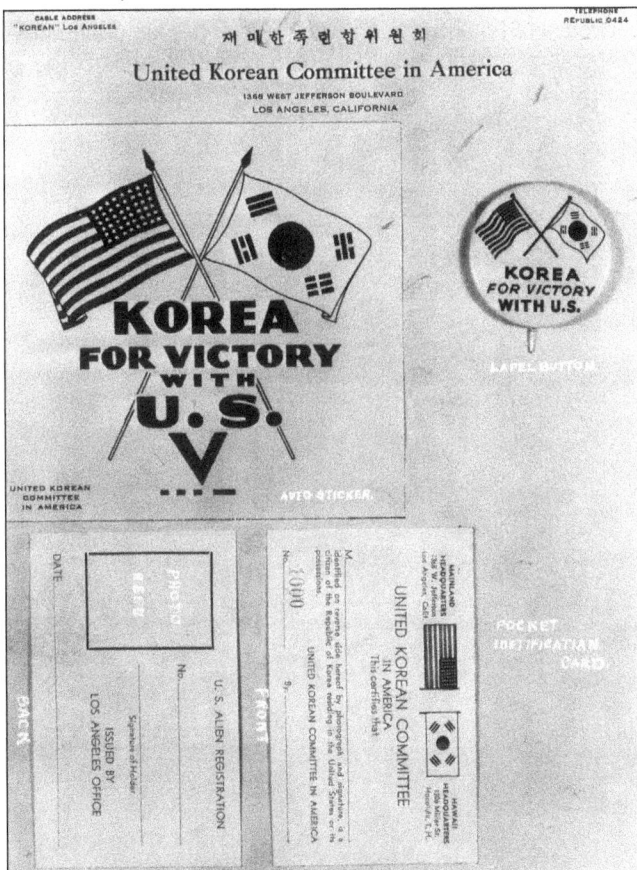

Members of the United Korean Committee, the executive committee, and delegates from Hawaii convened in Los Angeles in April 1942. They are photographed in front of the Korean National Association building at 1368 Jefferson Boulevard. (LAPL.)

미국가주나성시청에날느는한국국긔
여긔럽회치외국원九十二월八二대민一

The Korean flag raising ceremony at Los Angeles City Hall was held in recognition of Korea on August 29, 1942. The Tiger Brigade marched from Pershing Square to city hall and commemorated the first time that the Korean flag was officially flown in the United States. (KADA.)

The California Korean Reserve, nicknamed "the Tiger Brigade" (*Manghokun*), was photographed at the Los Angeles Exposition Park Armory in 1942. One-fifth of the Korean population in Los Angeles—around 109 men from the ages of 18 to 65—joined the California National Guard. They would meet for three or four hours on Saturdays and Sundays for drills to defend the state against enemy invasion. (KADA.)

The Korean American women's unit of the California National Guard practices drills at the Armory. The United Korean Committee funded these special Korean units to exemplify their patriotism to America. Two Tiger Brigade men, Henry Yoon (far left) and Yin Kim, are on the left. In the second row of women, on the far right, Carrie Yoon Kim Kwon stands in formation. (KADA.)

The 27th annual Young Korean Academy convened on Christmas Day, 1940, at 3421 South Catalina Avenue. (KADA.)

Four members of the Ahn family enlisted in the military during World War II. Ralph (left) was in the US Navy; Philip (center) was in the US Army; and Susan (right) was a lieutenant in the US Navy—the first Korean American woman in the American military and the first female gunnery officer. Not pictured in this 1944 photograph is their sibling Philson, who was a member of the California National Guard in the Tiger Brigade. (HAC.)

In 1941, Charles Yoon enrolled at the University of Southern California School of Dentistry. Unable to pay for his second year, he took a year off and started a partnership to run the produce section of the Dollar Markets in Long Beach. Many of the young Korean Angeleno men were able to find work there, as job opportunities were limited at the time. During his second year at USC, Yoon enrolled in the Army Special Training Program, a conscription program that enabled him to complete his education and then enlist in the Army or Navy. Yoon graduated in June 1944 and became a lieutenant in the US Navy. He went on to become the first Asian oral surgeon in Beverly Hills and taught at the USC School of Dentistry for 15 years. (KADA.)

Col. Young Oak Kim, born and raised in Bunker Hill, was awarded 19 medals, including the Distinguished Service Cross, two Silver Stars, two Bronze Stars, three Purple Hearts, a Bronze Medal of Military Valor, a *Légion d'honneur*, a Croix de Guerre, and (posthumously) the Korean Taeguk Cordon of the Order of Military Merit, for his service in World War II and the Korean War. After his retirement from the military, Kim became an Asian American activist, helping found the Go For Broke Monument; the Japanese American National Museum; the Korean Health, Education, Information and Research Center (KHEIR); and the Korean American Museum; among others. (Young Oak Kim Center for Korean American Studies.)

Florence Ahn was a Hawaiian-born soprano singer who came to Los Angeles in the late 1930s to study at Los Angeles City College. She performed in a number of musicals and operas across the city in the early 1940s. (KADA.)

Gloria Kim Hahn (wearing crown) was the Korean Queen of "I am American" day—a US bond fundraising event. She marches through Brookside Park near the Rose Bowl in Pasadena with her court, including Annabel (Lee) Kim at her left. (KADA.)

A May 20, 1943, article on Sammy Lee's graduation from Occidental College was in the English-language *New Korea*, a weekly newspaper published by the Korean National Association. At the time, Lee was already a national diving champion. The pool close to his home had both a springboard and tower, but people of color could only use it one day a week. It was reportedly emptied and filled with fresh water for the other six days. (Sammy Lee.)

NEW KOREA

d English Weekly in North America Estab lished 1910

LIFORNIA   Thursday, May 20, 1943

EEN' SOLD

AUCTION

KOREAN DIVING CHAMPION GRADUATES

Included among the 200 Seniors of Occidental College at Eagle Rock, Los Angeles, who received the degree of Bachelor of Arts at the fifty-first annual commencement of the college on the afternoon of May 17 was the nationally-known Korean diving champion.

He is none other than Samuel Lee, son of Mrs. Soon Ki Lee and the late Mr. Lee, at 1909 San Fernando Road, Los Angeles.

During his academic years at Occidental College Samuel endeared himself to the student body not only for his brilliant activities in sports but for his fine scholarship as well.

Holder Of National Diving Championship

The climax of his sports career as a swimmer was in August 1942, when he won the national diving championships in 33 feet tower in Columbus, Ohio, and 10 feet spring-board in New London, Conn. Both events were sponsored by the American Athletic Union with about 25 colleges and universities throughout the country participating in it. It not only the first time for the West Coast to bring the national diving championship but also Samuel is the first and only Oriental and Korean young man to have won such a coveted honor.

During his entire career as

SHORT-WAVE BROADCAST TO KOREA

Korean company K in San Francisco will broadcast short-wave (KGEI) a special program to Korea at 5:30 a. m. (San Francisco time) on Saturday May 22.

Swimmer Samuel has so far won more than 25 medals of all descriptions for his diving, for he has traveled across the country several times to demonstrate his superart of diving. It is said he starts his career as a diver about the school stage.

It is expected Samuel will enter the medical school of the University of Southern California a member of Army Reserve Corps this coming term.

It may be noted he is the younger brother of Miss Elizabeth Lee, graduate of the U. S. C. and now associate editor of the San Francisco Chronicle and Miss Mary Lee, also graduate of the U. S. C. and active member of the Korean Methodist church at 36 Normandie, Los Angeles.

The second generation comes of age. Two sisters, Emma (left) and Ada Park, are photographed in 1944. Their father, Kim Tak Park, was a minister in Delano. (LAPL.)

Bethuel Chung was born in Dinuba in 1925. After serving as a corporal in the US Air Force as an airplane mechanic and gunner during World War II, he moved to Los Angeles in 1948, the year this photograph was taken. He is pictured on his Indian 74cc (he said he couldn't afford a car at the time) in front of a Korean-owned rooming house at West Thirty-sixth Street near Vermont Avenue. He graduated from UCLA in 1958 with a bachelor of science degree in engineering, and he worked as an aerospace engineer for most of his life. (LAPL.)

Calla Lee and Bill Chunn are photographed at the popular Casino Gardens nightclub in Santa Monica in 1946. The club was frequented by Korean Americans for dancing. (LAPL.)

There were several weddings in the second-generation Korean American community in Los Angeles in the mid- to late 1940s. Harold Yoon and Gloria Insook Park (right) were married at the West Adams Presbyterian Church on Adams Boulevard in 1947. Young Tak Kim and Annabelle Lee (below) were another couple wed in 1947 in Los Angeles. Harold Yoon was in an antiaircraft battalion of the US Army and fought in Europe. On the day Pearl Harbor was bombed, Yoon said he heard the news on the radio as he was "shooting dice" at the back of Hank's Restaurant on Jefferson Boulevard. He and his brother Hongtak Kim enlisted shortly thereafter. Young Tak Kim was a radar man in the US Navy deciphering Morse code on a destroyer escort on the Pacific. The couples waited until the war was over to hold their weddings. (Both, KADA.)

A gathering at the Korean Presbyterian Church at 1374 West Jefferson Boulevard took place in 1944. Church membership in 1939 was 32, but 65 or 70 people would attend Sunday services, which were conducted in Korean. (HAC.)

The Korean Women's Patriotic League (*Taehanin Yoja Aeguktan*) was formed in 1919 in Dinuba, joining together the San Francisco Korean Women's Society, the Sacramento Korean Women's Association, and the Los Angeles Women's Friendship Association. Heyryon Ahn was the group's first president. The Korean Women's Patriotic League also aligned with the Korean National Association in the cause for Korean independence. They also raised funds and helped needy Koreans in the community. This is their 29th anniversary gathering in Los Angeles. (HAC.)

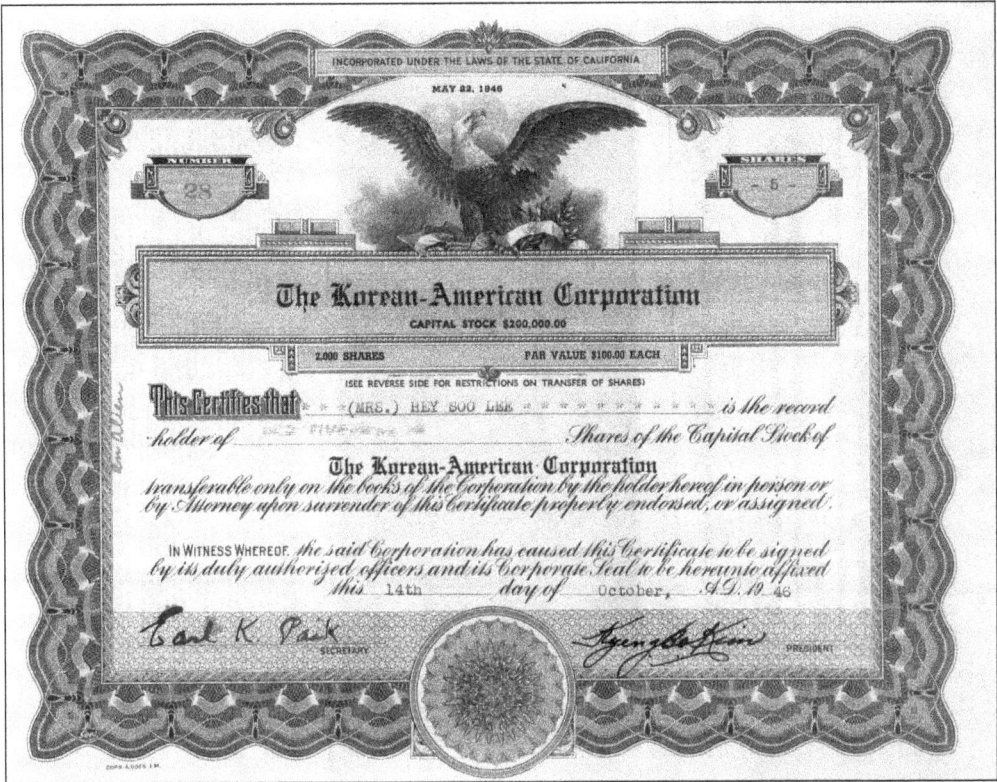

Above is a stock certificate made out to Hey Soo Lee for five shares of the Korean American Corporation on October 14, 1946. (KADA.)

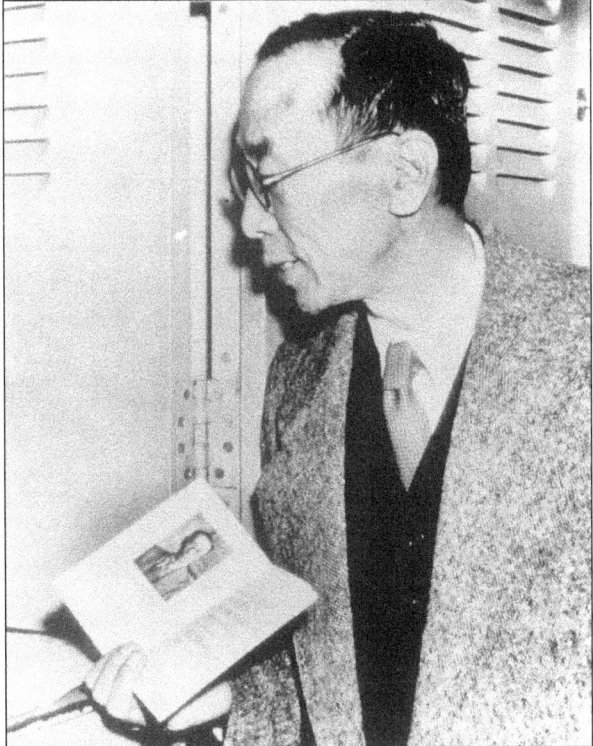

Dong Sung Kim was the president of the Korean Pacific Press, a publishing house, in 1946. The press published a pamphlet entitled *50 Facts on Korea*, which included maps and photographs. (KADA.)

Two Korean American tailors stand in front of a shop in 1945. Job opportunities were limited due to discrimination. There were approximately 73 Korean-owned businesses at the time and most were in fruit and vegetable stands, grocery stores, wholesale companies, trucking companies, restaurants, and laundry and pressing shops. (LAPL.)

This photograph is of a Song family dinner at a Korean herb shop in Los Angeles in June 1947. There were three Korean-owned herb shops at the time, where "herb doctors" worked prescribing herbal remedies for their clients, who were Korean, Chinese, Filipinos, and Americans. (LAPL.)

The Korean Methodist Church choir was comprised of about 20 members, and they were a well-known "outstanding group" in the community. They performed around Los Angeles at other Protestant churches and were broadcast several times on KFWB, a radio station in Hollywood. (KADA.)

The Korean Methodist Church holds its Easter Sunday service in 1950 at 1276 West Twenty-ninth Street in Old Koreatown. The church had seen many pastoral changes in the 1940s. Rev. Key Hyung Chang was its first bilingual pastor, serving from 1941 to 1947. Ha Tai Kim was pastor from 1947 to 1949 and Henry Chang-hee Oh from 1949 to 1953. (KADA.)

The Korean Presbyterian Sunday School (above) in 1949 was held at 1374 West Jefferson Boulevard and the Korean language school in 1950 was held at 1368 West Jefferson Boulevard at the Korean National Association (KNA) building. The church group would meet during the summers, with international student teachers. The KNA building was the community center at the time where social functions and club meetings were held. It was also referred to as the Korean Center. (Above, KADA; below, LAPL.)

Rev. Stewart Lim hands out certificates of completion for an Americanization class held at the Korean Presbyterian Church in 1951. At the time, foreign language services were being discouraged in the denomination. (LAPL.)

A reception for the Republic of Korea Navy was held in Los Angeles on March 19, 1952, during the Korean War. The uncertainty on the Korean peninsula and the coming-of-age of the second generation shifted the community towards settling permanently in the United States. (KADA.)

There were several second-generation youth clubs, such as the Zamburaks, the Outlaws, the Monarchs, the 2-8 Club, the Squires Club, the Ewha Club, the Girl Reserves, and the Young Korean National Academy. The Squires Club had basketball tournaments for boys ages 14 to 17. They held practices at the Korean Center twice a week, and the tournament proceeds went towards college scholarships for the community. The Tigers are photographed around 1950. They played against other Korean teams in California or local Chinese teams. (LAPL.)

Irvin Paik is photographed on his bicycle in front of his family home at 274 West Forty-first Street at Broadway in Old Koreatown in the early 1950s. (KADA.)

Hey Soo Lee's registration certificate shows her address in the Old Koreatown neighborhood. Korean nationals were still required to register. (KADA.)

樣式第二號
Form No.2

在外國民登錄證
REGISTRATION CERTIFICATE OF KOREAN NATIONALS

1. 姓名 李(金)慧壽 Full Name Mrs. Hey-soo Lee
2. 生年月日 一九0一年十二月三十一日 Date of Birth Dec. 31, 1901
3. 本籍 全羅北道 全州府 西井里 Permanent Domicile Ser Jung Ri, Chunju City, Cholla Pukdo, Korea.
4. 現住所 Present Address 226½ W. 46 Street, Los Angeles 37, Calif.
5. 外國民登錄番號 Alien Registration No. 2647055
6. 職業 아파-트 먼트 業 Occupation Apt. management
7. 滯留目的 居住 Purpose of Stay Alien resident
8. 本人의直屬家族 Registrant's Immediate Family

姓名 Full Name	生年月日 Date of Birth	關係 Relationship	性別 Sex	職業 Occupation
義英 (Edwin)	Sept. 7, 1928	Son	Male	軍人

此登錄證所持者는大韓民國國民임을證明함
I certify that the bearer of this Certificate is a national of the Republic of Korea

檀紀四二八四年 五月 一日
Date May 1, 1951

大韓民國 羅城 總領事舘
Republic of Korea Consulate General in Los Angeles, Calif.

副領事 Woonsang Choi
Woonsang Choi
Vice Consul
Signature and Seal

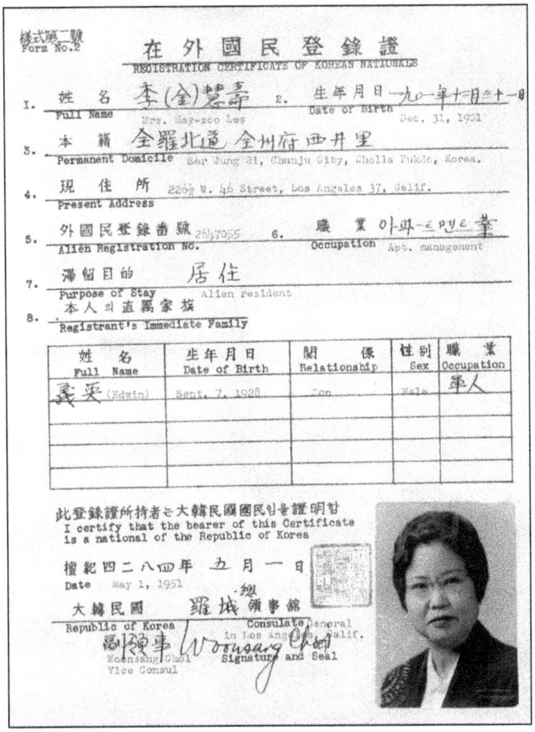

The 1953 naturalization certificate of Charles Yoon's mother, Do Yen Yoon (also known as Hazel Yoon), is pictured below. She was living in Delano, California, at the time, where there were several hundred Koreans farming produce. (KADA.)

THE UNITED STATES OF AMERICA

ORIGINAL
TO BE GIVEN TO
THE PERSON NATURALIZED

No. 7039772

CERTIFICATE OF NATURALIZATION

Petition No. 3567

Personal description of holder as of date of naturalization: Date of birth January 28, 1893 sex Female complexion Dark color of eyes Brown color of hair Black-gray height 5 feet 4 inches weight 120 pounds; visible distinctive marks None
Marital status Married former nationality Korea

I certify that the description above given is true, and that the photograph affixed hereto is a likeness of me.

Hazel Yoon
(Complete and true signature of holder)

State of California
County of Kern } ss:

Be it known, that at a term of the Superior Court of Kern County held pursuant to law at Bakersfield, California on November 18, 1953 the Court having found that HAZEL YOON then residing at 1614 Belmont Street, Delano, California intends to reside permanently in the United States (when so required by the Naturalization Laws of the United States), had in all other respects complied with the applicable provisions of such naturalization laws, and was entitled to be admitted to citizenship, thereupon ordered that such person be and (s)he was admitted as a citizen of the United States of America.

In testimony whereof the seal of the court is hereunto affixed this 18th day of November in the year of our Lord nineteen hundred and fifty-three and of our Independence the one hundred and seventy-eight.

Seal

Leva B. Gibson
Clerk of the Superior Court.

By ________ Deputy Clerk.

It is a violation of the U.S. Code (and punishable as such) to copy, print, photograph, or otherwise illegally use this certificate.

DEPARTMENT OF JUSTICE

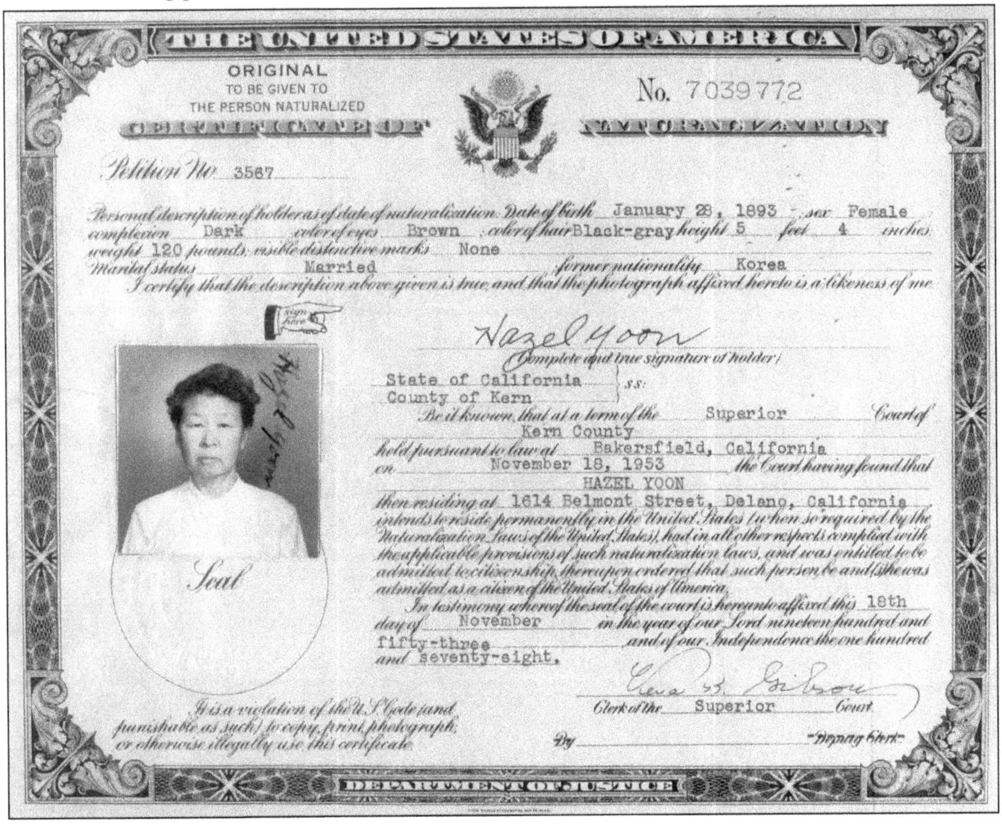

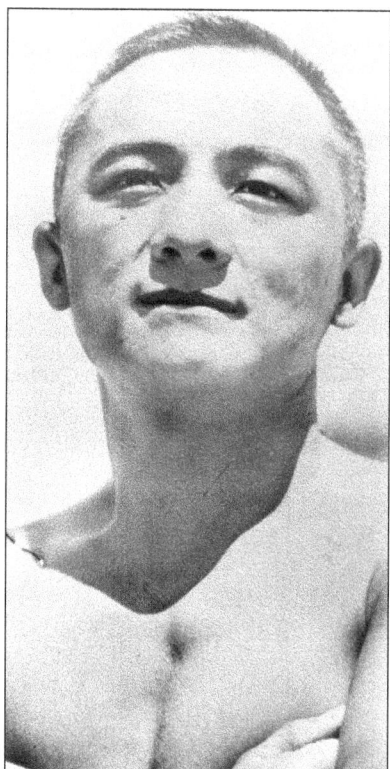

Sammy Lee (left) was the first person to win two gold medals in the Olympic platform diving event. He was also the first Asian American to win a gold medal. Because the Olympics were suspended due to war in 1940 and 1944, Lee had to wait until 1948 to compete. During that time, he graduated from the University of Southern California Medical School in 1947 and became a major in the US Army Medical Corps. Right before his event at the 1948 Olympics in London, Lee's teammate Miller Anderson (who won the silver) told him that his wife overheard a US official saying to the judges, "I hope you do not favor that Korean." Lee said he "dived with anger," and he won the gold medal in platform diving and a bronze in the springboard event. In 1952, he won the gold again in the platform event in Helsinki. Below, Lee is pictured with Syngman Rhee on September 20, 1953. Rhee was a close personal friend of Lee's family. (Both, KADA.)

Sammy Lee won the 1953 James E. Sullivan Award from the Amateur Athletic Union as the most outstanding amateur athlete in the United States. It was the first time the award was given to a person of color. Lee was notified of this honor while he was serving at the 121 Evacuation Hospital in Yong-dong Po as a major in the US Army Medical Corps during the Korean War. (KADA.)

The 50th anniversary of the Korean Methodist Church was held in Los Angeles in 1954. (KADA.)

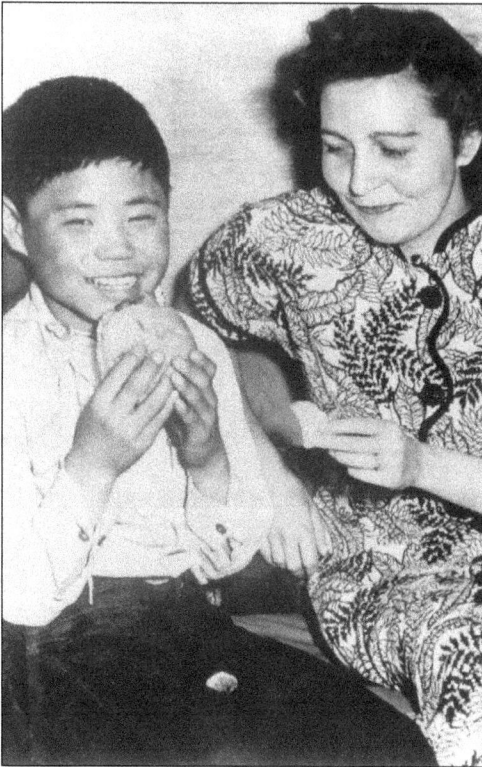

Song Yong Cho, a Korean War orphan, is photographed on May 25, 1953, with his adoptive mother. There were 14,027 Koreans who immigrated to the United States during the Second Wave, from 1950 to 1964. This number was directly related to the Korean War and its aftermath. Of that number, 6,423 were wives of American servicemen, or "G.I. brides;" 5,348 were war orphans; and the remaining 3,256 were students or professional workers. The orphans were raised in mostly middle-class suburban families. They were also sent to Western Europe, Canada, and Australia. As the adoptions began in 1950, many of those children have reached adulthood, and their fate has become a national issue in South Korea, as many Koreans felt ashamed at what they saw as an abandonment of their children. In the 1990s, homeland tours were organized so adoptees could return to South Korea to learn about their native culture. In October 1998, Pres. Kim Dae Jung invited 29 Korean adoptees to the Blue House and publicly apologized for their plight and the government's inability to raise them in Korea. (Left, KADA; below, LAPL.)

The 41st Assembly of the Young Korean Academy was held in front of its headquarters at 3421 South Catalina Avenue in 1955. (KADA.)

This is an April 17, 1955, gathering of the Korean Presbyterian Church at 1374 West Jefferson Boulevard to celebrate the church's deacons and elders. (KADA.)

Luther Hahn, son of pioneer Si Dae Hahn, and his family are photographed in front of their gas station in Inglewood in 1956. (KADA.)

Soorah and Philip Ahn opened Phil Ahn's Moongate Restaurant in Panorama City in 1955 at 8632 Van Nuys Boulevard. As one of the first Chinese restaurants in the San Fernando Valley, it stayed open for 30 years. By the 1950s, Ahn had a celebrated acting career, having played dozens of roles—often Chinese and Japanese characters—on film. In May 1962, he was named Honorary Mayor of Panorama City. (HAC.)

The 50th anniversary of the Korean National Association is photographed in front of the 1368 West Jefferson Boulevard headquarters on February 1, 1959. (KADA.)

Three third-generation siblings, Russell (left), Leslie, and William Yoon, are pictured in front of their house on Mascot Street in 1960. (KADA.)

The 43rd anniversary of the Korean Women's Patriotic League was held on August 5, 1962. (KADA.)

American Korean Civic Organization

4328 DON DIABLO DRIVE • LOS ANGELES 8, CALIFORNIA

EXECUTIVE OFFICERS
FOR 1963

EDDIE PAIK
PRESIDENT

GEORGE OH
VICE-PRES.

HENRY YIM
2D VICE-PRES

YOUNG MAN KWON
TREASURER

CLARENCE LEE
ASST. TREAS.

ANITA YIM
CORRES. SECY

ESTHER PAIK
RECORDING SECY

•

ALFRED H. SONG
LEGAL ADVISOR

GEORGE OH, C.P.A
AUDITOR

•

BOARD OF DIRECTORS

CHARLES YOON, D.D.S.
CHAIRMAN

•

STANLEY CHOY
JULIA HALM
WILLIAM HERR. D.D.S.
THOMAS HONG
CHARLES KIM
GEORGE KIM, D.D.S.
YOUNG MAN KWON
CLARENCE LEE
HENRY LEE
RAYMOND LEE
VIRGINIA LEE
WILLIAM R. LEE
PHILLIP LYOU
GEORGE OH
EDDIE PAIK
ESTHER PAIK
ARTHUR PARK
HENRY YIM
KEN YOON
DAVID KIM
WOONHA PARK

•

ADVISORY BOARD

REV. YOUNG YONG CHOI
DR. PETER S. HYUN
CHANG HA KIM, M.D.
CHARLES HO KIM
REV. H. L. KIM
LESTER E. KIM, B.D., PhD.
SAM LEE, M.D.
S. T. RYANG, M.D.
WALTER CHANG HO SHIN
JOHN K. HAN
LEO SONG

•

Dr. Charles Yoon
1st president

After World War II ended, a meeting was held to reconvene the Young Korean National Association. Dr. Charles Yoon felt that the Young Korean National Association, as a subsidiary of the Korean National Association (KNA), might exclude those in the second generation whose parents were not members of the KNA. He founded the American Korean Civic Organization in 1962. Yoon was the organization's first president. (KADA.)

Mayor Sam Yorty was the first official to meet with the American Korean Civic Organization in 1962 at a dinner (above). The AKCO later met with Gov. Ronald Reagan and Gov. Pat Brown. The group also presented a gift to Elizabeth "Betts" Yorty (below). (KADA.)

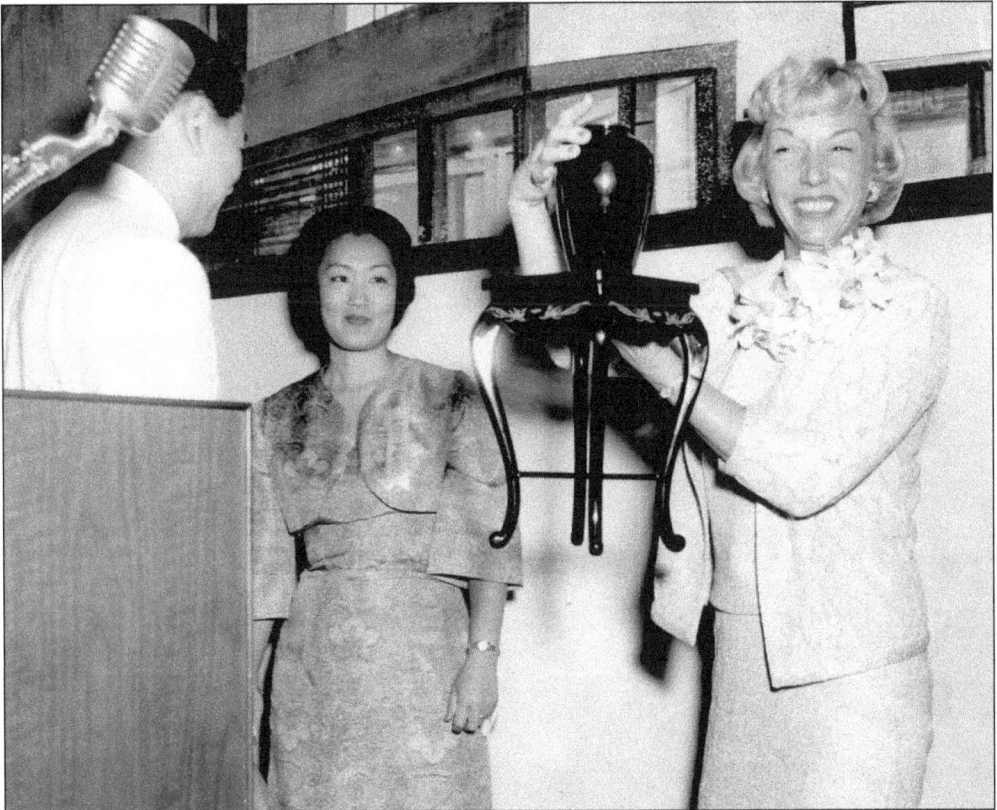

Philip Ahn (left) and Sam Yorty worked together in 1969 on the Los Angeles–Pusan sister city affiliation. Ahn was the chairman of the committee. (HAC.)

In this 1968 aerial photograph of Koreatown, Wilshire Boulevard runs west-to-east. The tall building at the center left of the photograph was the Travelers Insurance Building at 3600 Wilshire Boulevard, built in 1960 at the intersection with Ardmore Avenue. Today, it is the Nara Bank building. The building in the center, on the far right, was the Sheraton Wilshire Motor Inn, which is now the Wilshire Hotel. (USC.)

Korea House was the first Korean restaurant in Los Angeles. It was built by Francis Lewe at 2731 West Jefferson Boulevard in 1965. Prior to this, Koreans ran Chinese-style restaurants. For Korean groceries, many shopped at the Great Eastern Industrial Company, which was located at 4716 South Normandie Avenue. There were also Japanese-run markets near the intersection of Normandie Avenue and Jefferson Boulevard in the 1940s that sold fresh tofu. It was cut up and placed in cigarette cartons or ice cream boxes. There were reports of a woman who lived on Forty-third Street and Normandie Avenue in the West Adams district who made homemade *kim chi* for the community. (KT.)

The Y&Y (Yoon and Yim) Market was opened in the early 1950s at Union Avenue and Eleventh Street in the Pico-Union district by Young June "Junie" Yoon and Hank Yim. It was a neighborhood grocery and liquor store. Y&Y eventually closed in the 1980s. (KADA.)

The *Korea Times* opened its Los Angeles headquarters in 1969 in Studio City in the San Fernando Valley. Key-Young Chang founded the parent publishing company, Hankook Ilbo, in Seoul. His son Jae Min Chang (below, right) is the chairman and chief executive officer of the *Korea Times* Los Angeles, and another son Jae Ku Chang is the chairman of the *Hankook Ilbo-Korea Times* Media Group in Korea. Today, the *Korea Times* is the largest Korean-language newspaper in the United States. There are nine bureaus in the United States, two in Canada, and one in Argentina and Brazil, respectively. (Both, KT.)

Four

KOREATOWN

Olympic Market was a renowned Korean grocery store that opened in Los Angeles in October 1971. Hi Duk Lee, a real estate developer, built the market at the corner of Olympic and Harvard Boulevards. Koreans from as far as San Diego would make the weekly trek to get Korean produce and groceries. (Hi Duk Lee.)

The VIP Palace (*Young Bin Kwan*), a Korean restaurant at 3014 West Olympic Boulevard, opened on May 25, 1975. It was the brainchild of Hi Duk Lee, who also built the adjacent shopping center, the VIP Plaza. They were both built in traditional Korean-style architecture—a first in Los Angeles. Lee imported more than 10,000 blue tiles from Korea to roof the complex. On July 25, 1975, Lee (below, right) is pictured in front of grand opening bouquets holding his oldest daughter, Susan. His wife is on his right and his brother and sister-in-law are to his left. (Both, Hi Duk Lee.)

Hi Duk Lee, who is a descendant of the Lee Royal Family in Korea, was one of the first visionaries in Los Angeles's Koreatown. He arrived in the United States in 1968 with plans of creating Koreatown. He had first immigrated to West Germany, where he was a miner; his wife was a nurse. Throughout the 1970s and 1980s, he was the director of the Koreatown Development Association, the Koreatown Chamber of Commerce and the Korean-American Friendship Association. He brought "Koreatown" signs to the 10 Freeway and the neighborhood. While he was planning the VIP Hotel in the late 1970s, high interest rates and his tenants defaulting on their rents forced Lee to declare bankruptcy. He sold everything in 1982. Currently, the former VIP Palace is an Oaxacan restaurant called La Guelaguetza. (KT.)

Sonia Suk arrived in Los Angeles in 1962 and became the first Korean realtor in Southern California. She was one of Koreatown's early leaders and served in more than 60 Korean American organizations in Los Angeles and throughout the United States. She was appointed by Mayor Tom Bradley to the Los Angeles Human Relations Commission in 1976 and served for eight years. (KT.)

The *Korea Times* offices move from Studio City to Koreatown in 1971. The new offices were located at 3418 West First Street between Virgil and Vermont Avenues. At the time, there were approximately 10,000 Koreans in Los Angeles. (KT.)

The Korean Association of Southern California was established on Olympic Boulevard on March 27, 1972. Pictured are, from left to right, Kyo Sook Lee, Song Kil Chang, Jee Choe Cho, Robert Lee, Key Soon Kim, Kwang Jae Kim, and Han Kyo Kim. (KT.)

世界最初 太平洋横断 B747 貨物専用機 就航
Inauguration of World's First Transpacific Service by B747 F

대한항공 태평양 화물노선 취항식(1971년 4월 26일). 첫 화물기 보잉707이 4월 26일 김포를 이륙, 도쿄를 거쳐 LA 국제공항에 도착한다는 소식이 전해지자 100명이 넘는 한인들이 공항에 나가 환영했다.

A ribbon-cutting ceremony commemorates the inauguration of Korean Airlines cargo service in the United States. The transpacific flight took the 747 from Seoul to Los Angeles on April 26, 1971. (KT.)

L·A 공항에 태극기 물결
80세 교포 눈물글썽 8·15이후 두번 째 감격

환영객들 혼란 빚기도
이곳저곳서 계획 계때 안알려

The first Korean Airlines passenger plane made its arrival at the Los Angeles International Airport on May 16, 1973, at 10 p.m. There were 280 passengers aboard. According to the International Air Transport Association, Korean Airlines had 20.41 million passengers and moved 1.57 million tons of cargo in 2009. (KT.)

The Oriental Mission Church first opened in Los Angeles in 1970 at the pastor's residence. On January 26, 1975, the nondenominational church moved to a former Ralph's supermarket location at its current 424 North Western Avenue home. At the time, there were around 150 Korean churches in the area. Today, there are more than 3,000 Korean American churches in the United States—1,200 in California alone—and many of them provide critical social services, as well as a sacred space for faith and community. Although figures widely vary, approximately 80 percent of Korean Americans are tied to the Protestant church, 11 percent with the Roman Catholic church, and 5 percent with Buddhist temples. Below, five graduates are pictured at the Korean Youth Center in 1975. The graduates are, from left to right, (first row) Mi Kyung Nam; (second row) Bo Kyung Chi, Chul Koh, In Chul Hong, and Young Wook Kim. (Left, author; below, Korean Youth and Community Center.)

Sung Hee Lee (center) was crowned the queen of the First Annual Southern California Miss Korea pageant in 1975. Hee Jong Yang (left) came in second place and Myung Hee Lee came in third. (KT.)

Young Woo Kim deejays the first Korean-language radio broadcast, *Jung Ja Suh*, in the Southern California area on October 12, 1974. There are currently three radio stations in the Los Angeles area that broadcast entirely in Korean: KMPC (Radio Korea), KYPA, and KFOX. (KT.)

A street view of Koreatown in 1976 displays the blossoming of Korean businesses in the neighborhood. The large sign at the top advertises a department store (*baek hwa jum*). Other signs displayed are for gift shops, cosmetic shops, and restaurants. (KT.)

The High Society custom tailor shop opened on March 25, 1968. It was one of the first Korean businesses to open on Wilshire Boulevard. The owner, Richard Lim, arrived in Los Angeles in 1961 and initially worked as a dishwasher and manual laborer. At first, High Society catered to the Korean and Korean American community, but word of his bespoke suits traveled, and he began tailoring for the Hollywood elite. His business is still open in its original location. (KT.)

In the early 1970s, the third generation of Korean Americans comes of age. Here, Bill Yoon (his grandparents are pictured on page 14 and his parents are on page 61) is photographed in 1972 at the Taquitz Pines campground near the city of Idyllwild. Yoon owns Koreana Gifts and Art, a gift shop with Korean wares, near the intersection of Crenshaw and Washington Boulevards. (KADA.)

The Park family pays heed to their family's gravesite at Rosedale Cemetery at 1831 West Washington Boulevard in the West Adams district. It was opened in 1884 and was the first cemetery available to all races and creeds. Many of the early Korean Angelenos are buried here. In 1993, it was renamed the Angelus-Rosedale Cemetery. (KADA.)

The Third Annual Korean Parade, sponsored by the *Korea Times*, is held on Olympic Boulevard in 1976. The parade is part of the Los Angeles Korean Festival, which has been held annually since 1974. In 1999, the Los Angeles Korean Festival Foundation was organized, overseeing the event, which gathers more than 400,000 visitors to one of the largest ethnic celebrations in the nation. (KT.)

Fr. Matthew Ahn of the St. Nicholas Episcopal Church in Hollywood offers assistance to recent Korean immigrants on August 15, 1977. In 2001, the *Korea Times* reported that the 16 largest Korean churches in Los Angeles had more than 31,000 members with a $52.1 million budget. (LAPL.)

90

Veteran Korean American journalist K.W. Lee launched *Koreatown*, the first Korean American English-language weekly, in 1979. At right is the cover of the first issue of the first volume. Lee, who came to the United States in 1950, was best known for his six-month investigative coverage of the Chol Soo Lee case, in which a Korean American immigrant was wrongfully imprisoned for a murder in Chinatown. Chol Soo Lee was later released in 1983. (K.W. Lee.)

The Koreatown Development Association—formed on February 21, 1973, by Jin Hyung Kim, among others—holds its monthly "sweep-in," a street cleaning beautification campaign, in 1980. Around 250 members participated and cleaned Olympic Boulevard between Western and Vermont Avenues. This photograph is at a bus stop at the intersection of Olympic Boulevard and Normandie Avenue. (LAPL.)

A demonstration in 1980 depicts the Koreatown community's continued involvement in homeland politics. In May 1980, the South Korean army killed over 100 civilians at a pro-democracy uprising in Gwangju, a city in southern Korea. Residents in Koreatown held a protest at Seoul International Park at the intersection of Olympic Boulevard and Irolo Street. (KT.)

They're assimilated, but still Korean

200 at weekend reunion reflect on the world of their fathers

By Colleen Monica
Herald Examiner staff writer

When Edwin Lee tried to rent an apartment near Crenshaw Boulevard and Santa Barbara Avenue in 1955, he was turned away despite the big "Vacancy" sign outside.

His sister Rose Shur and her husband were trying to buy a house in Pico Rivera about the same time, but also were rejected. They ended up in Compton, one of the "acceptable" neighborhoods for Asians.

About a year ago the Shurs' son Tim bought the townhouse he wanted in West Covina. He had no problem greater than getting together the down payment.

"I think the old prejudices my mom and uncle talk about have almost disappeared — they exist but to a lesser extent," said Shur, who at 33 is an officer in the Los Angeles Police Department.

The three family members sat in a banquet room at the Ambassador Hotel yesterday, reflecting on the experience of being American-born Koreans. They were among about 200 Koreans and people of Korean ancestry attending a weekend convention.

The family stressed that being American-born Koreans, their lives are much different from those of Korean immigrants. For one thing, the immigrants tend to live in enclaves where Korean is spoken and cultural heritage is maintained.

Neither Tim Shur nor Lee, 51, a computer engineer from Canoga Park, speaks Korean. Mrs. Shur, 56, a Gardena resident, remembers only a few words from her childhood. When Tim and her other son Douglas, 32, also a Los Angeles police officer, were growing up, the family spoke only English, she said.

They no longer live in what was the Korean neighborhood near 37th Street and Western Avenue where Mrs. Shur, Lee and their three siblings grew up. They were children of immigrants who came from Korea in 1912 and 1917.

One of the reasons for the convention was to hold a reunion of these old friends, "to come together before we all disappear" through assimilation, said Dr. Richard Hahn of Belvedere, one of the organizers.

There is no formal organization of American-born Koreans, and Hahn said the convention was the brainchild of his wife Gloria, a former Los Angeles resident.

An August 31, 1980, *Los Angeles Examiner* article is headlined "They're assimilated, but still Korean." The article reports on a convention attended by more than 200 Korean Americans at the Ambassador Hotel and remarks upon the discrimination felt by the first generation lightening for the more-assimilated second generation. (KADA.)

The Korean Cultural Center opened in 1980 at 5505 Wilshire Boulevard in the Miracle Mile district. The mission of the center, run by the Ministry of Culture, Sports, and Tourism, is to promote the cultural heritage of Korea. The KCC has a museum and library and offers Korean-language classes and free school tours to Los Angeles Unified School District students. The adjacent Korea Center was opened in 2006. (KT.)

Two Korean American juvenile delinquents stand trial in this 1980 photograph. Youth gangs in Koreatown began to form in 1974, with the organization of the "AB" (American Burger), "Old Boys," and "Hollywood Boys." The rest of the decade into the 1980s saw an intensification of crimes from fistfights to armed robbery and murder. Overworked parents, racial discrimination, and difficulty in schools were among the major factors contributing to the alienation of these youth. (KT.)

Korean immigrants in Los Angeles in the 1970s were largely an educated group, however, their prestigious degrees and professional experience did not transfer in the United States. Compounded by language barriers and discrimination, many white-collar professional opportunities were unavailable. As a result, in the late 1980s, almost 40 percent of Korean men in Los Angeles owned their own businesses. Liquor stores in low-income neighborhoods were popular because of the low capital required to start up the enterprise, as well as the lack of competition and low-maintenance customers. Within the "ethnic enclave economy," family or informal associations led to leads and loans, and the success of greengroceries and liquor stores—not to mention the autonomy and the ability for the entire family to work—was appealing. South Central Los Angeles in particular was a food desert following the Watts Riots. (Both, KT.)

The Koreatown Police Community Center opened in 1981 as a storefront on Eighth Street. At the time, a federal task force had been established to investigate Koreatown crime syndicates. The Los Angeles Police Department created this center to have police presence in the neighborhood. (KT.)

On September 1, 1981, Korean Air Lines Flight 007 was shot down as it strayed into Soviet airspace over the East Sea, west of the island of Sakhalin. All 269 passengers and crewmembers aboard the New York-Anchorage-Seoul flight were killed. Korean liquor store owners in Los Angeles boycotted liquor from the Soviet Union. (KT.)

The Korean American Federation (*Han in Hoi*) of Los Angeles originally started out as the California Korean Center in 1962 by immigrants who wished to create a social network in their new country. This photograph shows the federation leadership with a sign declaring the new name in 1982. Today's mission remains to ease transition into the United States, to be a liaison to the mainstream, and to be leaders in the Korean American community. The federation is linked to other branches across the country and is generally regarded as an organization for first- and 1.5-generation Koreans (a label for Korean Americans who were born in Korea and immigrated at a young age), both in its history and interests. (KT.)

Swap meets were popular Korean businesses in Los Angeles in the 1980s. Modeled after the *Namdaemun* and *Tongdaemun* markets in Seoul, the swap meets had a number of stalls in an indoor or outdoor open space. (KT.)

The Consulate General of the Republic of Korea in Los Angeles is located at 3243 Wilshire Boulevard on New Hampshire Avenue. The first Korean consular office in the United States was opened in Los Angeles in 1948. (KT.)

Chinese Koreans in Koreatown represent the Korean diaspora. Many Koreans emigrated first to South America, China, and West Germany before resettling in the United States. Currently, the Koreans in China outnumber the Koreans in America. (LAPL.)

On January 12, 1982, a "Koreatown" sign was placed on the Santa Monica Freeway at the Normandie Avenue exit. Mayor Tom Bradley (fourth from left), Koreatown Development

Association president Hi Duk Lee (far right), consul general Min Soo Park, and California Department of Transportation director Peter Oswald were among those present. (KT.)

The Koreatown Plaza was the largest project to date in Koreatown when it broke ground in 1984 (above). It took almost four years to build the $25-million, three-level indoor mall (below), developed by Joong Nam Yang and designed by Ki Suh Park of Gruen Associates. In 1984, according to the then-Korean Chamber of Commerce, more than 60 percent of the 7,000 Korean-owned stores in Los Angeles County were located outside of Koreatown. At 227,000 square feet, the Koreatown Plaza opened in January 1988, housing a large supermarket, a food court, a bank, and more than 80 retail stores, symbolizing the movement for Koreatown's growth in the 1980s. (Both, KT.)

A group of newly naturalized citizens of the United States hold up their certificates in 1984 at the Los Angeles Convention Center. The Office of Immigration Statistics in the US Department of Homeland Security reported that 17,576 South Koreans were naturalized in 2009. Interestingly, it was the first year that North Korea was included in the yearbook, with 28 naturalizations. (KT.)

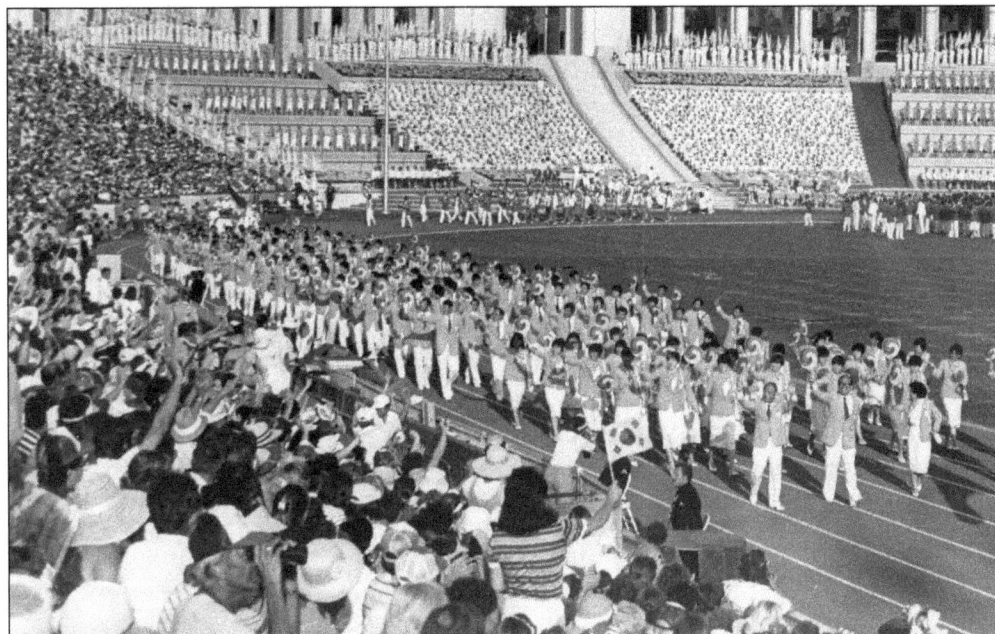

The Korean community cheers and welcomes the Korean Olympic team during the opening ceremonies of the Games of the XXIII Olympiad held at the Los Angeles Memorial Coliseum in 1984. (KT.)

The Immigration and Control Act of 1986 granted amnesty to illegal immigrants who had entered the United States before January 1, 1982, and had lived in the United States continuously since their arrival. Families reunited at the Los Angeles International Airport in June 1988. Kyu Nam Kim (right) was able to see his wife, Jong Sun Yoo, after years of separation. The law, also known as the Simpson-Mazzoli Act or Senate Bill 1200, also included certain illegal agricultural workers. More than three million illegal immigrants received amnesty, however, due to widespread fraud, it has been regarded as a failed legislation. (KT.)

Philip Ahn posthumously received a star on the Hollywood Walk of Fame on November 14, 1984. (He died in 1978.) The star is located at 6207 Hollywood Boulevard near the Pantages Theatre between Vine Street and Argyle Avenue. From 1955 to 1978, he appeared in numerous television series, such as *Bonanza*, *Hawaii Five-O*, MASH, and *Kung Fu*. In his lifetime, he amassed 180 titles as an actor. He is the only person of Korean descent to have been awarded a Hollywood star. (HAC.)

Three men relax at a strip mall, at 955 South Vermont Avenue, that is typical of the architecture of many stores and restaurants in Koreatown. In this 1986 photograph, the mall included *Ham Kyung Do*, a restaurant famous for its blood sausages (*soondae*), an acupuncturist, an accountant, and a locksmith. (LAPL.)

A Korean strip mall emerged in the San Fernando Valley in 1985. Many Koreans who immigrated in the 1970s initially lived in Koreatown but relocated to suburbs such as Garden Grove, Glendale, and Diamond Bar when it became financially feasible. According to the 2000 census, out of the 345,882 Koreans in California, 55,573 lived in Orange County—a nearly 55-percent increase from 1990. (KT.)

Esther Lee became the first female Korean American graduate of the Los Angeles Police Academy on February 21, 1988. (KT.)

The Venerable Pope John Paul II and his motorcade ride through the 13th annual Koreatown Parade at the Los Angeles Korean Festival on Olympic Boulevard on September 19, 1987. (KT.)

Olympic Market closed its doors in 1988. The restaurant Suhrabal went in its place. In May 2007, the owner was shot and killed in the restaurant in an apparent murder-suicide. (KT.)

A billboard advertises Arthur Song's 1987 campaign for the 10th Council District of the City of Los Angeles. He eventually lost to Nate Holden, who held the office from 1987 to 2003. There are 15 districts in Los Angeles; Koreatown falls under four city council districts and five state assembly districts. This fracture became significant after the 1992 riots, when elected officials deflected responsibility for recovery efforts, claiming other districts were liable. Currently, there is a push in the community to draw new redistricting lines to unify a political voice for the community. (KT.)

Representative Chang-jun "Jay" Kim (third from left) of the 41st congressional district was the first Korean American elected to the US Congress in 1992. He later pleaded guilty to accepting $230,000 in illegal donations (including campaign contributions) and was fined and sentenced to two months of house arrest. (KT.)

Five

THE LOS ANGELES RIOTS

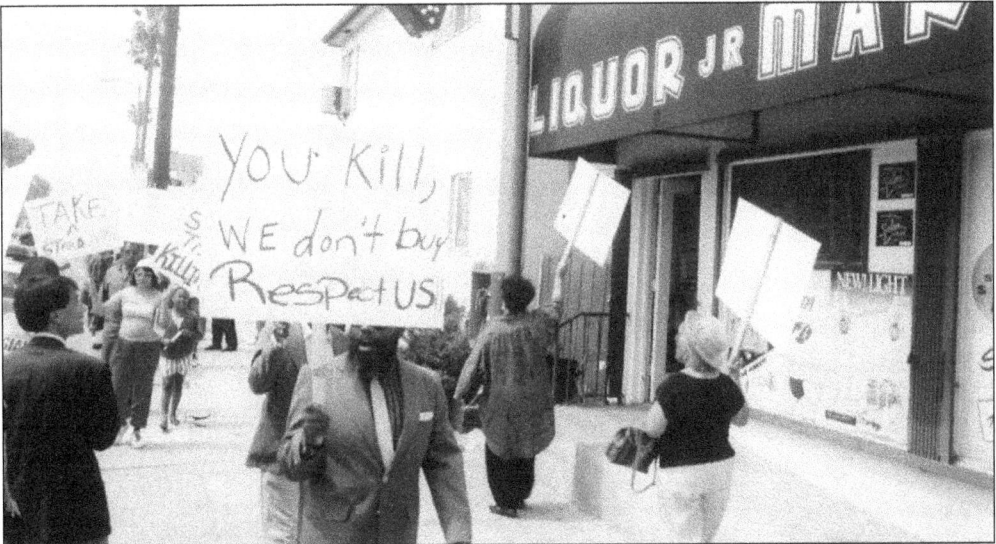

Protesters boycott a Korean-owned liquor store in June 1991. On March 16, 1991, Empire Liquor Market owner Soon Ja Du shot and killed 15-year-old Latasha Harlins in South Los Angeles. Du, believing that Harlins was trying to steal a bottle of orange juice, grabbed the girl. An altercation ensued and Harlins was shot in the back of the head inside the store. Although Du was found guilty of manslaughter, Judge Joyce Karlin reduced her sentence to probation, infuriating the African American community. This incident led to widespread boycotts of Korean-owned stores and is believed to be a catalyst for the destruction to Koreatown during the 1992 Los Angeles riots. (KT.)

On the evening of March 2, 1991, African American motorist Rodney King led police through a high-speed car chase in the San Fernando Valley. Four white Los Angeles Police Department officers were videotaped beating King as he was being apprehended. After seven days of deliberation, the jury acquitted the four officers of assault on April 29, 1992. The riots began that evening. (KT.)

An African American man holds up a sign saying "We will not rest" as a fire burns in the background. After the verdict was read at the Simi Valley Courthouse at 3:15 p.m., protests started almost immediately at the courthouse, then later at the Los Angeles Police Department headquarters and the intersection of Florence Street and Normandie Avenue in South Central Los Angeles. Outnumbered in South Central, the Los Angeles Police Department retreated and violent attacks and looting began. (KT.)

Although the riots were largely regarded as a "Black-Korean conflict," more than half of the approximately 12,000 arrested were Latino. Widespread looting occurred on all three days of the riots. Crowds of looters swarmed on Korean-owned stores in Koreatown. An unknown man (above) steals a sofa. (KT.)

A Korean man on his phone assesses the damage. Due to a lack of community leadership and police presence, Radio Korea broadcasted pleas for volunteer security to help community businesses. Armed militias led by former South Korean marines responded. (KT.)

Forever etched in people's memories is the image of Korean vigilante store owners, armed with rifles on the roofs of their buildings, protecting their property. While for some it signified the community's resilience, for others it perpetuated a stereotype of Koreans as ruthless, xenophobic, and self-serving. The media coverage fanned the incident as an interethnic conflict between Koreans and African Americans, ignoring at its heart the history of injustices that both communities have endured. (Both, KT.)

An armed officer points his shotgun. During the first and second days of the riots, there was little to no police protection. Korean shop owners repeatedly called the Los Angeles Police Department for help, before turning to Korean-language radio stations. By the middle of the second day, the police and fire department began to respond, and Mayor Tom Bradley called for a curfew. By the third day of the riots, thousands of California National Guard troops, federal law enforcement, and local police patrolled the riot area. By Saturday, May 2, another 4,000 soldiers and Marines arrived from Fort Ord and Camp Pendleton. (KT.)

Though reports on the damage vary widely, more than 3,500 fires had been set over the course of the riots and approximately 1,100 buildings were burned. At least 53 people died during the riots and more than 2,000 were injured. (KT.)

A Korean woman is in tears while being interviewed. More than 50 percent of the 3,100 Korean American businesses in Los Angeles were damaged or destroyed at an estimated cost of $350 million. Total estimated damages vary from $700 million to $1 billion. (KT.)

According to the Korean American Grocers Association, a mere six out of 170 Korean-owned stores that were destroyed in South Central during the riots were reopened by January 1994. Many Koreans were not insured (or were fraudulently insured) and lost their life savings. Consequently, many Koreans moved out of Los Angeles and into the suburbs. (KT.)

More than 30,000 people rallied at a peace march on May 2, 1992. (The Korean media estimated the crowd at 100,000.) Though the Los Angeles riots left the Korean American community visibly scarred, it was also a political awakening for Korean Americans. Signs reading "Rebuild Koreatown," "Why Me Why Korean," and "Peace Love" are seen among the crowds. (KT.)

The only victim of Korean descent was Edward "Eddy" Jae Song Lee (pictured), an 18-year-old who was responding with three of his friends to a call for security on Radio Korea on the second night of the riots. As Lee and his friends arrived at the Kang-Suh-Myon-Oak noodle house, they were pulled from their car and shot in the crossfire. The funeral for Lee was held at Forest Lawn Cemetery after a street memorial service where he was shot and killed. There was also a community funeral service at the Ardmore Recreation Center in Koreatown. The portrait held by a family member and wrapped in black ribbon follows traditional Korean funerary customs. (KT.)

The Koreatown Emergency Relief Committee was established in the aftermath of the riots to assist the Korean Americans whose businesses were damaged or destroyed. Bags of rice and canned food are being distributed at the Oriental Mission Church on Western Avenue. (KT.)

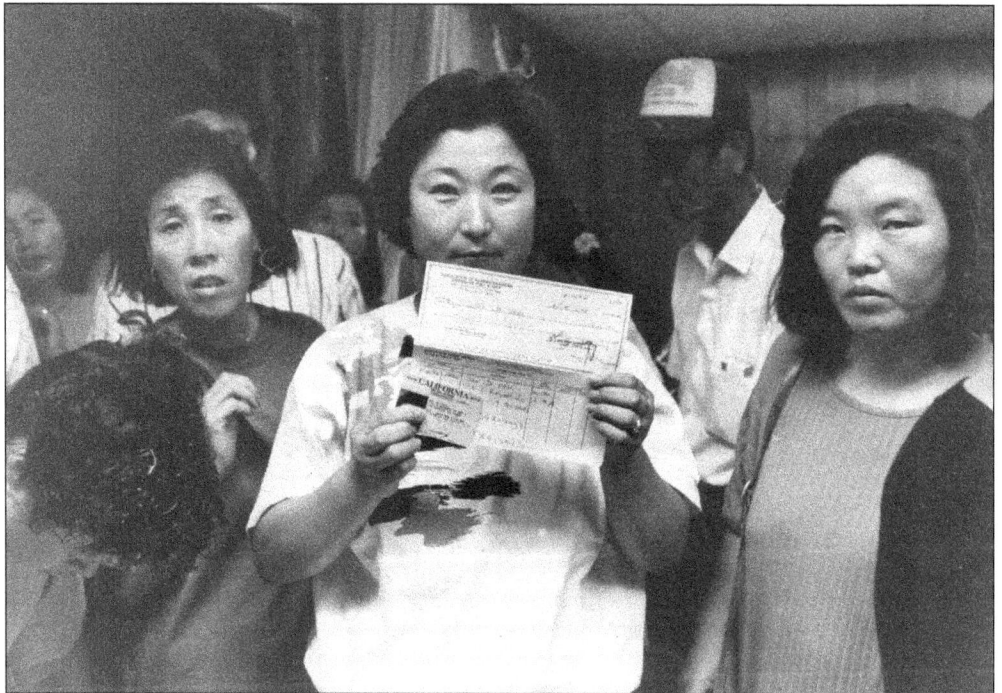

A Korean woman holds up her distribution check from the Association of Korean American Victims of the Los Angeles riots. (KT.)

114

Six

REBUILDING AND THE FUTURE

South Korean investment during the 1990s contributed to the rebuilding of Koreatown after the 1992 Los Angeles riots. The Aroma Wilshire Center, located at Wilshire Boulevard and Serrano Avenue, is a $35-million spa, 150-yard golf range, and mall built by the South Korean Hanil Development Company. A lifetime membership to the spa—modeled after high-end sports clubs in South Korea and targeting affluent Korean Americans—cost $22,000 to join when Aroma opened in 2001. These large-scale transnational ventures transformed the visual landscape of Koreatown from small mom-and-pop shops to multileveled modern shopping centers, condominiums, and office buildings. (KT.)

Chan Ho Park signed with the Los Angeles Dodgers as an amateur free agent in 1994 when he was a sophomore in college. He pitched for the Dodgers for seven years, and returned again for another year in 2008. In 2011, he is playing for Nippon Professional Baseball. (KT.)

A labor union in Koreatown pickets for restaurant workers' rights. In 1996, the Korean Immigrant Workers Advocates (KIWA) started the Restaurant Workers Justice Campaign. At that time, more than 97 percent of the Korean restaurants in Koreatown were noncompliant with California labor standards, such as fair wages, overtime, and workers' safety. KIWA faced opposition from Korean organizations such as the Korean Restaurant Owners Association, which could not understand why a Korean American organization would picket one of its "own." The rift represents differences in the ideologies between some in the first and second generations and is significant in how Koreatown politics in the 21st century will be conducted. (KT.)

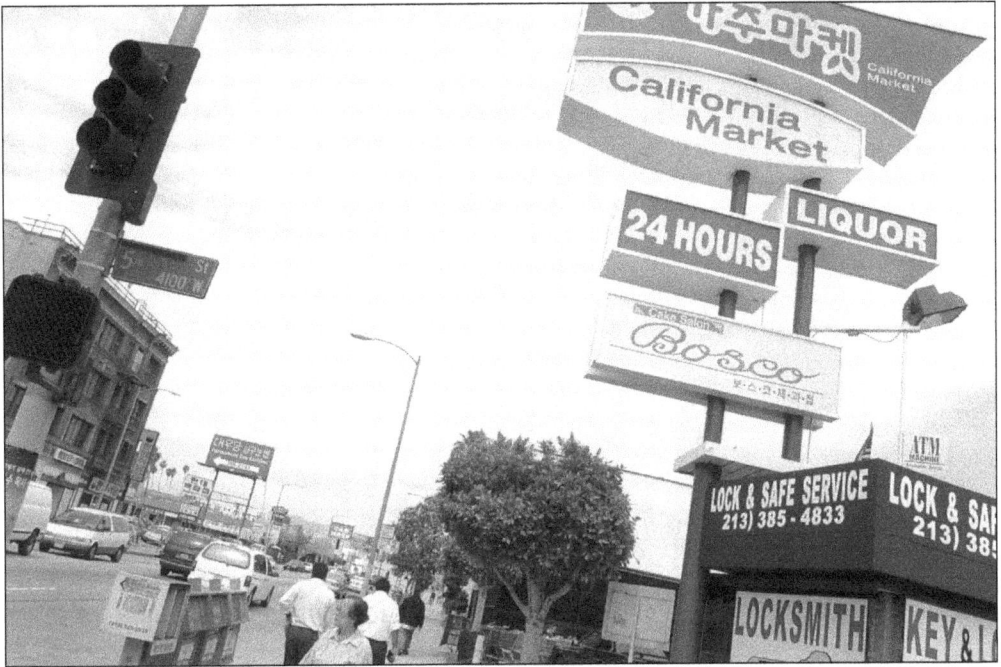

California Market, on Western Avenue and Fifth Street, was the site of one of the armed encampments during the riots. Store owner Richard Rhee, along with several men, stood on the rooftop armed with automatic weapons and shotguns. Rebuilt and thriving, this photograph shows the 24-hour Kaju Market in 2000. (KT.)

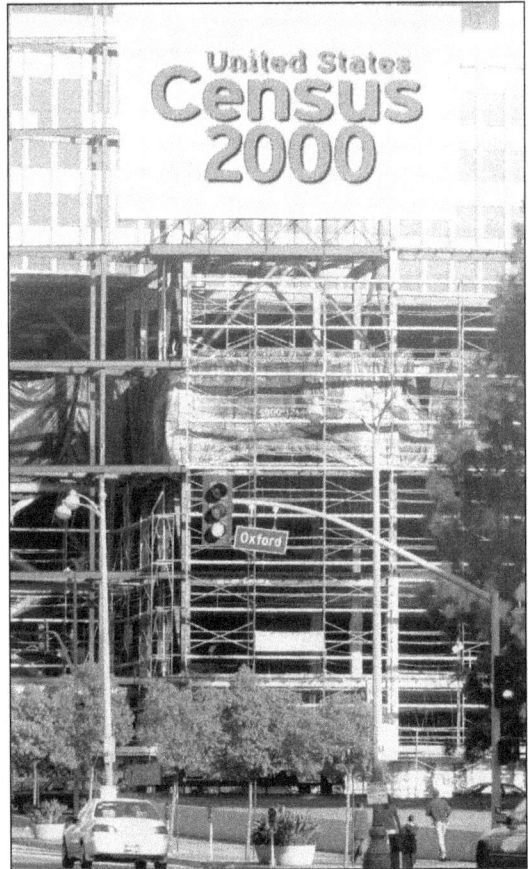

A sign for the US Census 2000 is placed along Oxford Avenue. The 2000 Census counted 1,076,872 Korean Americans in the United States; Los Angeles County accounted for 186,350. In Koreatown alone, there were 46,664 Koreans. (KT.)

A typical strip mall in Koreatown displays that despite the movement of Korean Americans to the suburbs, Koreatown still remains the business center of the community. Many of the signs are still in *Hangul*, which has been alienating for some in the mainstream population of Los Angeles, but connotes an ethnic pride among Korean Americans. This photograph from 2000 shows signs for a bedding shop, a bakery, a café, a video store, a comic (*manwha*) reading room, an optometrist, and a barbershop. (KT.)

One of the many medical office buildings in Koreatown is at 2727 Olympic Boulevard. According to the Korean American Medical Association of Southern California, there are approximately 700 physicians in Los Angeles and Orange Counties. Helen Givens, in her USC master's thesis on the Korean community in Los Angeles, accounted for two Koreans in Los Angeles County practicing medicine in 1939. Nearly 40 percent of Koreans in America do not have health care. (KT.)

In 1929, the Chapman Market opened on Sixth Street and Alexandria Avenue as the world's first drive-in grocery store. With its restaurants, coffee shops, and karaoke bar, Chapman Plaza (above, in 2002) has become a popular nightspot in Koreatown. The ornate Spanish Colonial Revival building was restored in 1989 by the Ratkovich Company, an urban development firm that specializes in rehabilitation projects in Southern California. Ratkovich also completed renovations for the Wiltern Theater (right) in 1985, and despite the architectural beauty and popularity of both venues, both were financial failures for his firm. After the 1992 riots, Wilshire Boulevard underwent a $6-million urban renewal project, Streetscape, which oversaw the planting of more than 2,000 trees. The Metro Red Line opened in 1996, connecting Wilshire Boulevard to downtown Los Angeles, Long Beach, Hollywood, Universal City, and the Los Angeles International Airport. (Both, KT.)

Jamison Properties started acquiring office buildings on Wilshire Boulevard in 1995. Dr. David Lee, a Korean American internist from the San Fernando Valley, came to the United States when he was 17 years old. His father owned a grocery store in Koreatown. With Lee at the helm, Jamison Properties—with its original coterie of Korean and Korean American backers—has become one of Southern California's largest commercial real estate firms with a portfolio of more than $3 billion. (Author.)

Ten years after the 1992 Los Angeles riots, a commemorative march was held on Olympic Boulevard. Korean Americans at the rally carry a large American flag and signs calling for peace. From 1992 to 2002, businesses in South Central invested more than $1.4 billion in the area, yet unemployment remained in the neighborhood at around 20 percent. (KT.)

In 2003, numerous ceremonies and parades were held to commemorate the Korean Centennial—the 100th anniversary of the arrival of the SS *Gaelic* in Hawaii. (KT.)

The Pio Pico–Koreatown Branch of the Los Angeles Public Library (LAPL) reopened in 2002 after an extensive remodel at 694 South Oxford Avenue, one block south of Wilshire Boulevard. It holds the largest Korean language collection in the LAPL and is its Korean Language Resource Center. The name "Pio Pico–Koreatown" was approved by the board of library commissioners in 1990, when Korean American patronage to the library had increased to more than 50 percent. (KT.)

Susan Ahn Cuddy and Ralph Ahn hold a sign commemorating the Dosan Ahn Chang Ho Memorial Interchange on the 10 and 110 Freeways on June 11, 2004. California senator Kevin Murray of the 26th district, who sponsored the sign naming, is standing on the right. (HAC.)

In September 2004, a US post office was named the Dosan Ahn Chang Ho Station at 3751 West Sixth Street (at the intersection of Harvard Street). The House of Representatives, led by Rep. Diane Watson of California's 33rd Congressional District, unanimously signed the bill on April 20, 2004. It was the first time a federal building was named after a Korean. Pictured from left to right are unidentified, Watson, councilmember Herb Wesson (District 10), Ralph Ahn, Susan Ahn Cuddy, and councilmember Tom LaBonge (District 4). (HAC.)

The Dosan Ahn Chang Ho Family House was moved in 2004 from its original location on Downey Way to Thirty-fourth Street on the University of Southern California campus. It was the house that the Ahn family lived in when they heard news of Chang Ho Ahn's passing in 1938. Since its relocation, the 2,000-square-foot building has been occupied by the USC College Korean Studies Institute. (Author.)

The intersection of Olympic Boulevard and Normandie Avenue was named Dr. Sammy Lee Square, in honor of the two-time Olympic gold medalist, on August 5, 2010. Lee (center), who was 90 years old at the ceremony, still swims six days a week. (KT.)

MY BROTHER NEED NOT BE IDEALIZED OR ENLARGED IN DEATH BEYOND WHAT HE WAS IN LIFE; RATHER HE SHOULD BE REMEMBERED SIMPLY AS A GOOD AND DECENT MAN, WHO SAW WRONG AND TRIED TO RIGHT IT, SAW SUFFERING AND TRIED TO HEAL IT, SAW WAR AND TRIED TO STOP IT.
— EDWARD M. KENNEDY

The former site of the Ambassador Hotel has been transformed into the Robert F. Kennedy Community Schools complex, where six pilot schools educate more than 2,400 students. The pilot schools control their own budgets, curricula, and staffing but are part of the Los Angeles Unified School District. Due to its hefty $578-million price tag, making it the most expensive public school in US history, it has been labeled a "Taj Mahal" school. The school opened in September 2010. (Author.)

In late 2008, a group of Bangladeshi Americans filed for an official designation of "Little Bangladesh" to cut a wide swath in the heart of Koreatown. Korean American organizations immediately realized they never had an official designation, despite blue street markers—in place since 1981—heralding the boundaries of the neighborhood. Korean Angeleno leaders petitioned for a three-mile area to be determined "Koreatown." For several months, there were heated debates between the ethnic communities of Koreatown and concerns from longtime Angelenos about the problems and complexities of ethnic flag-planting. Councilmembers Tom LaBonge (District 4, second from left) and Paul Krekorian (District 2, far right) are photographed with community leaders from Koreatown and Little Bangladesh. (Tom LaBonge.)

124

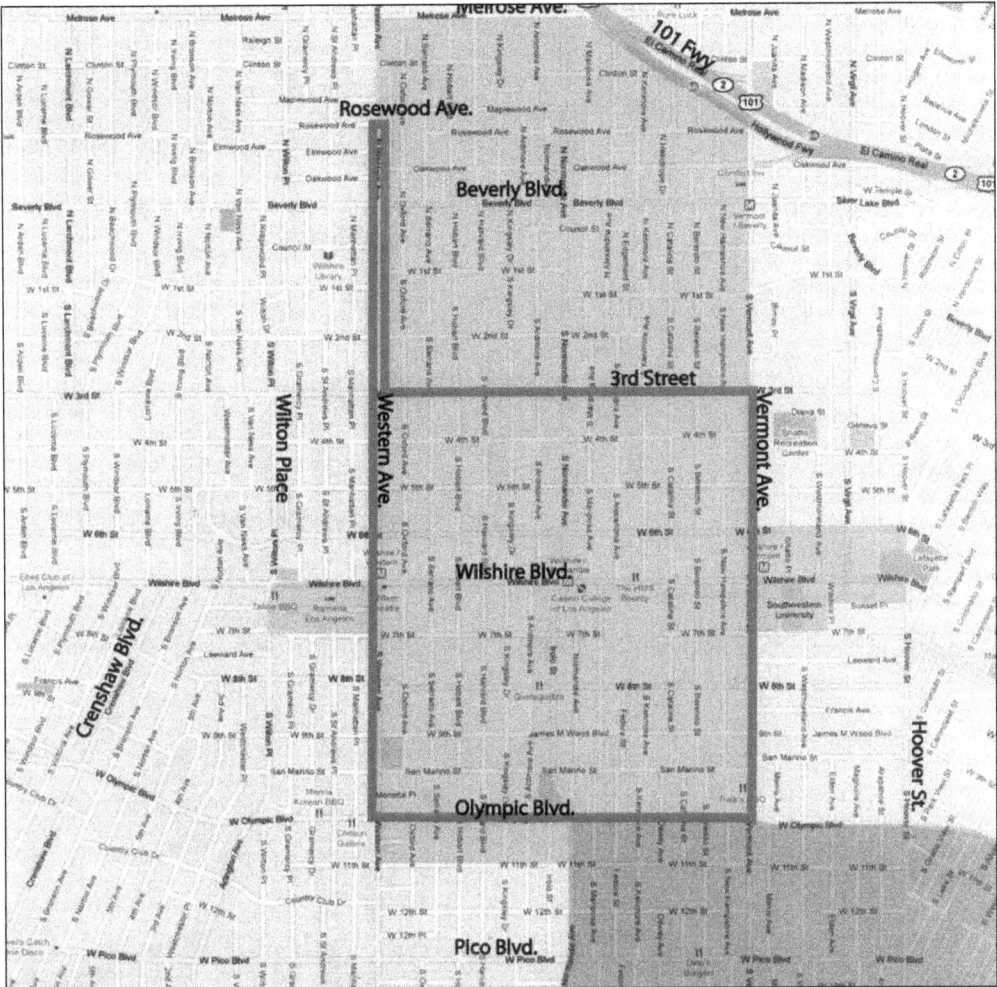

The new boundaries for Koreatown are Third Street to the north, Vermont Avenue to the east, Olympic Boulevard to the south, and Western Avenue to the west, including a narrow strip of Western Avenue up to Rosewood Avenue. Of its approximately 150,000 residents (though numbers widely vary, and many of Koreatown's residents do not participate in the census), more than 50 percent identify as being Mexican and Central or South American while more than 20 percent are Korean. Thirty percent are white, and around five percent are African American and Filipino, respectively. (Community Redevelopment Agency, Los Angeles.)

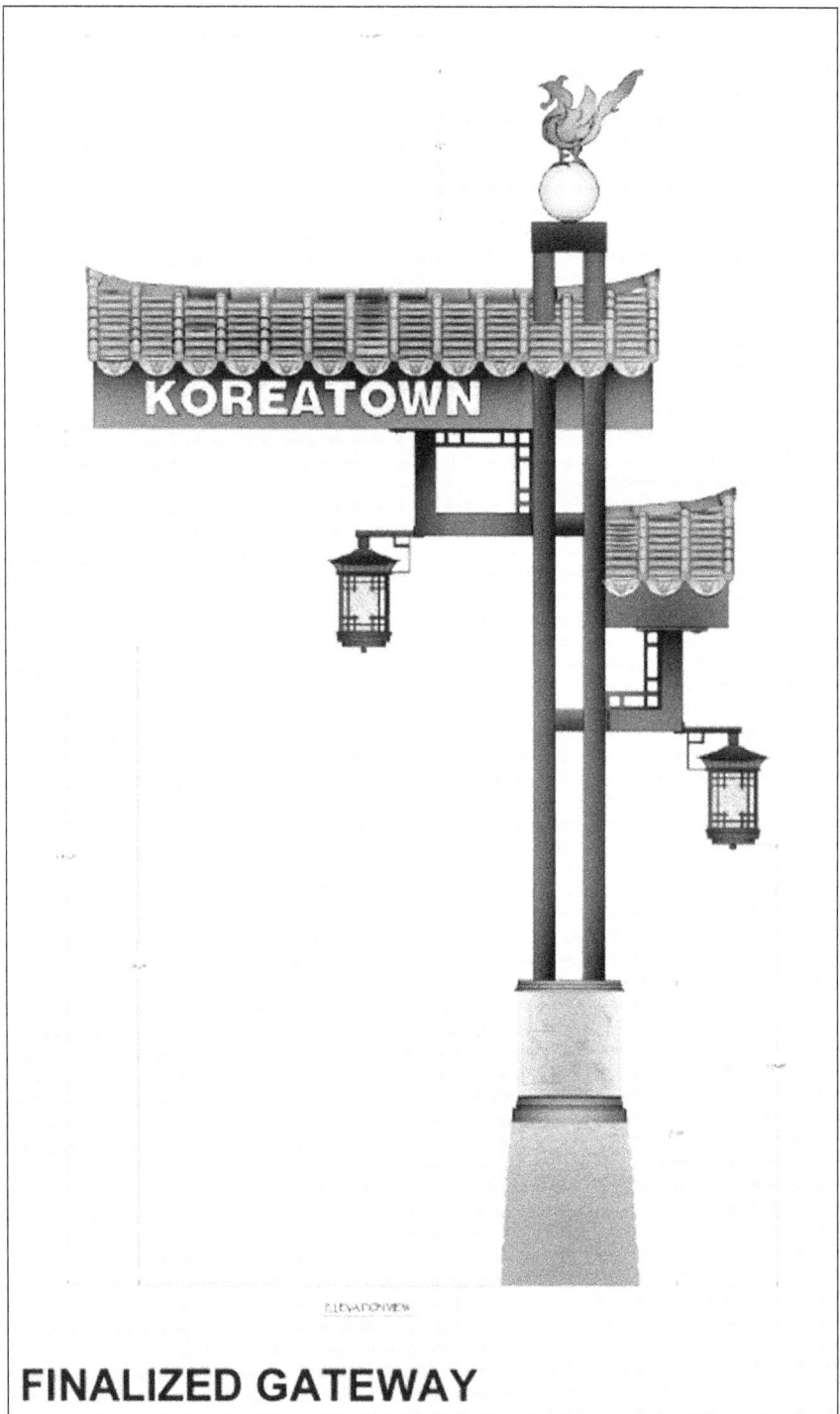

FINALIZED GATEWAY

Traditional-style Korean gates are being built on Olympic Boulevard at Vermont Avenue to the east and Western Avenue to the west. The streetscape project will also include planters in the medians to improve the lack of green space in the city. A park is also being constructed at Hobart Boulevard and Seventh Street. Both projects are slated for completion in 2012. (CRALA.)

BIBLIOGRAPHY

Abelman, Nancy and John Lie. *Blue Dreams: Korean Americans and the Los Angeles Riots*. Cambridge: Harvard University Press, 1995.

Ahn, Hyung Ju and David K. Yoo. *Faithful Witness: A Centennial History of the Los Angeles Korean United Methodist Church (1904–2004)*. Los Angeles: Kwang Jin Kim, 2004.

Cha, John. *Willow Tree Shade: The Susan Ahn Cuddy Story*. San Francisco: Korean American Heritage Foundation, 2002.

Cha, Jong Whan. *Pictorial Book of the Korean Immigration to the USA*. Los Angeles: *Korea Times*, USA, 2004.

Chung, Angie Y. *Legacies of Struggle: Conflict and Cooperation in Korean American Politics*. Stanford: Stanford University Press, 2007.

Given, Helen L. *The Korean Community in Los Angeles County*. MA Thesis. University of Southern California, 1939, Print.

Hurh, Won Moo. *The Korean Americans*. Westport: Greenwood Press, 1998.

Lee, Hi Duk. *Koamerican Maeari*. Seoul: Yangjongsa, 2006.

Lee, Mary Paik. *Quiet Odyssey: A Pioneer Korean Woman in America*. Seattle: University of Washington Press, 1990.

Roderick, Kevin. *Wilshire Boulevard: Grand Concourse of Los Angeles*. Santa Monica: Angel City Press, 2005.

Yu, Eui-Young, Earl H. Phillips, and Eun Sik Yang, eds. *Koreans in Los Angeles: Prospects and Promises*. Los Angeles: Center for Korean-American and Korean Studies, 1982.

Yu, Eui-Young and Hyojoung Kim, Kyeyoung Park, and Moonsong David Oh. *Korean American Economy & Community in the 21st Century*. Los Angeles: Korean American Economic Development Center, 2009.

Visit us at
arcadiapublishing.com

www.ingramcontent.com/pod-product-compliance
Lightning Source LLC
Chambersburg PA
CBHW050650110426
42813CB00007B/1967